EAST ANGLIA
SHIPWRECKS

EAST ANGLIA
SHIPWRECKS

STAN JARVIS

COUNTRYSIDE BOOKS
NEWBURY, BERKSHIRE

Also by Stan Jarvis:
Smuggling in East Anglia 1700–1840
Hidden Essex

First Published 1990
© Stan Jarvis 1990

COUNTRYSIDE BOOKS
3 Catherine Road
Newbury, Berkshire

ISBN 1 85306 111 5

Front cover illustration: Print by C. Hullmandel after a painting by William
Joy. It shows the Lowestoft Lifeboat *Frances Ann* attempting a rescue from a
wreck on the Holm Sand in 1820.

Produced through MRM Associates Ltd, Reading
Typeset by Acorn Bookwork, Salisbury
Printed in England by J. W. Arrowsmith Ltd., Bristol

Acknowledgments

Dredging up the details of shipwrecks through history and selecting the right ones for this book has required much research in many places where the custodians of the records have been so helpful that I must record my gratitude to:

The staff of the Chelmsford Library

The staff of the Essex Record Office

Jane Dansie, Local History Subject Specialist, Colchester Library

The staff of the Great Yarmouth Local History Collection

H.M. Coastguard, Great Yarmouth

Mr Richard Hawkins, Coxswain of the Gorleston lifeboat

Mr R. C. Temple, author

Mr R. R. Aspinall, Museum in Docklands Project of the Museum of London

Meg Davis-Berry, Editor, Essex Countryside

Chris Edwards, Radio Caroline

Essex County Newspapers

Ken R. Rice, Editor, East Anglian Daily Times

Mr D. Wright, Local Studies Librarian, Lowestoft

Peter Lake, Resources Librarian, Canvey Island Library

Anne Kirkby, Librarian, Essex Chronicle

I make special mention of two old friends without whom I could not have produced the photographs – Geoff Baker and Ron Patient.

The book itself could not have been researched and written without the help and companionship of my wife, Hazel.

Stan Jarvis
July 1990

Contents

Down to the Sea in Ships

There is no doubt that some ships have been wrecked off the East Anglian coast through human error. Yet only the people who sail boats, small or large, can appreciate how puny is the sailor and his ship when the wind blows up. The difficulties of navigation under a spread of canvas on a well-laden merchant ship can hardly be imagined today. There were so many days, running into weeks, when the wind was blowing from the wrong direction and at such great strength that hundreds of trading vessels were held up in port. When out on the deep the ship had no choice but to face the storm, trim the sails to ease its passage or turn and run for the nearest shelter in a port or off a headland.

Fleets of ships, fishing vessels in particular, could be wrecked wholesale by furious storms which changed the position of the sandbanks the fishermen had known for years like the backs of their hands. So nature's fury put the sailing ship in far greater and more frequent danger than ever did the occasionally inattentive or misguided mariner. In such storms the later steamships and motor vessels were just as much the toys of the elements.

In September 1671 around 76 ships are reckoned to have been wrecked off East Anglia. Masters of ships sailing after the storm were told to watch out – there was so much wreckage floating offshore that it could cause yet more damage. On just one awful night in 1692 no less than 200 ships and more than a thousand men went down in the Wash and along the North Norfolk coast. On Christmas Eve 1739, 16 ships were driven ashore between Yarmouth and Lowestoft. Another Christmas-time disaster occurred on 18th December 1770 when the wind suddenly changed from southwest to northwest and blew with such severity off the Suffolk coast that no cable or anchor was strong enough to hold a ship against it. Eighteen vessels were blown out of the safe channels and on to the dreaded sandbanks where they were broken up by towering waves raised by the wind over the shoals. Other ships were simply overwhelmed in the open sea.

In 1789 at least 130 fishing smacks and coasters were sunk or wrecked between Cromer and Southwold. Would-be rescuers were totally frustrated as they stood on the beach and looked across the raging seas to shout words of encouragement to seamen who had taken to the rigging of a doomed vessel. Another great wave would come pounding in and when they looked again the rigging was empty. The long list of casualties after the storm in February 1807 included the Yarmouth-based Revenue Cutter *Hunter*, out on anti-smuggling patrol. It was driven into the shallows off Winterton and every man jack of the crew died as it broke up in the terrible seas. The number of dead seamen washed up on the beaches was counted in hundreds. The loss of the Revenue Cutter *Ranger* in another storm in 1822 has been described in *Smuggling in East Anglia*.

In February 1877, a northwesterly gale with winds up to 87 m.p.h. hit a fishing fleet of up to 40 smacks from Yarmouth and Lowestoft manned by a hundred or so men. Not a single smack, or a single man, was ever seen again.

Two warships, the *Valorous* from Spithead and the *Seamew* from Woolwich, were sent to cruise the North Sea in search of possible survivors. Local smacksmen volun-

10

teered to go with them, to help with their practical knowledge. They were landed back again at Yarmouth on 2nd May. No trace at all had been found. The local paper reflected local feeling; '... it is all but certain that the hundred or so fishermen who were at sea in that ill-fated fleet have all, tempest driven in a terrible sea, found a watery grave ... it were like 20 shipwrecks, each with its own story of suffering, despair and death ... They have probably gone down without one to tell the story of their death. We may sympathise with those who are left, and can understand something of the feverish anxiety with which the wives and children, the mothers and sisters, of the missing men waited for their return, how their hearts day by day grew sick as the loved ones they looked for came not.'

So the long list could go on through another 130 years, culminating in the more recent manifestation of nature's violence, the great storm of 1953, which caused as much chaos, heartbreak and death on land in severe flooding as it did at sea. Ships, by now steel-strong and self-propelled, were better able to withstand the hammer blows of wind and wave. But that did not prevent the *Olcades* from being brought ashore at Walcott. It was an oil tanker 144 yards long and 19 yards broad – by far the biggest ship ever to have hit the Norfolk coast.

Out of this awful panorama of shipwreck we can only choose the merest selection to illustrate the seamanship and steadfastness of men doing their best to keep the trade lanes open in all weathers, and the gallantry and indifference to their own safety of the smacksmen and lifeboatmen who made every effort to rescue those seamen in their peril.

As to the awful experience of shipwreck there can hardly be a better short account than that from the pen of William Falconer (1732–1769), the barber's son who

went to sea, was shipwrecked in 1762 and, turning poet,
wrote his long poem, *Shipwreck* including:

'The ship hangs hovering on the verge of death,
Hell yawns, rocks rise, and breakers roar beneath! . . .
In vain the cords and axes were prepared,
For every wave now smites the quivering yard;
High o'er the ship they throw a dreadful shade,
Then on her burst in terrible cascade . . .
Again she plunges! hark! a second shock
Bilges the splitting vessel on the rock –
Down on the vale of death, with dismal cries,
The fated victims shuddering cast their eyes . . .
Ah Heaven! – behold her crashing ribs divide!
She loosens, parts, and spreads in ruin o'er the tide.'

Adrift in the Swin

The Swin is the channel running northwest from the
Thames estuary to the old Sunk lightvessel. It is bordered
by such dangerous sandbanks as the East and West Barrow, Maplin and Foulness sands, the Gunfleet and the
Sunk sands. A ship in the Swin could be like a man in a
maze, who could so easily lose all sense of direction. What
is more, the forfeit for losing one's way was too often
shipwreck and death by drowning or exposure.

Imagine the scene on a cold, Sunday morning in February 1739, long before dawn, when the old, wooden brigantine the *Ann*, sailing down the east coast, was almost in
view of its destination, the port of London. There was only
a reasonably safe, short journey up the Thames to be
undertaken before it could unload its cargo of corn, eggs
and salmon brought all the way from Berwick-on-Tweed.

One of the crew took a lantern and clambered down
into the bilges to check all was well. It was not, there was a
lot of water there. He hurried on deck to tell the captain.
Captain Steele took no risks, he looked for himself and
found the old ship had sprung a leak between the timbers
below the waterline. It was so severe that he gave the order
to heave to and start pumping. So they put out two
anchors to hold the ship just off the Black Tail beacon, in
those days stationed on the Blacktail Sand, with the Maplin sands on the other side of the channel. Then he
ordered all hands to the pump.

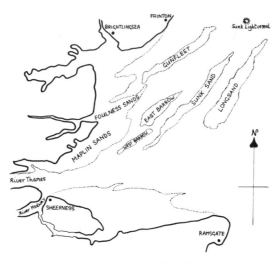

Sketch map showing the dangerous maze of sandbanks surrounding the Swin Channel where the brigantine *Ann* foundered in 1739.

For eight hours the crew of 13 cranked the pump handles continuously; but they saw the water winning all the way. They were exhausted, disheartened, just too worn out to carry on. So Captain Steele tried a desperate remedy. He ordered the cables to be slipped, sacrificing the anchors and the lengths of cable paid out to them, so that she was free in a moment. Free, the captain hoped, to drift with wind and tide on to the shallows, to be left high and dry when the tide receded, where they could hope for rescue in daylight by a passing ship. The trouble was that the *Ann* was now so heavy with water that it was barely moving, might sink any moment, and it seemed all was lost.

The captain made another move. A look-out had reported a light ahead, a long way off, so he had the ship's boat lowered and said he would take eight men with him, as many as the boat would safely hold, in an attempt to reach the ship that showed the light. He left the remaining

14

five crew members on board, telling them to put a light in the foretop and let the ship drift so that he could find it again in the dark if he was fortunate enough to get help quickly.

Then into the longboat he stepped. The men, already worn out with pumping, now bent their backs to chase that pinpoint of light which might mean rescue and relief for them all. The light slowly resolved itself into the shape of a German trader from Hamburg. As they came alongside and scrambled aboard their longboat sank under them. Captain Steele asked his fellow captain if he could borrow his longboat and go back for the remainder of his crew. The German captain refused categorically. He pointed out that as it was still dark and he was in dangerous waters, he and his crew might need that boat at any moment. 'We begg'd and pray'd, but he obstinately deny'd', wrote the captain later in his report. So he and most of his crew, safe on the German ship, had to watch helplessly as the *Ann* drove on before wind and tide for five hours. From dawn they watched, until their ship with their messmates finally went aground on the Westborough Sand – or West Barrow as we would call it today. They saw their ship hit the shallows and fall on its side under the battering of the waves. Their thoughts were all with those five shipmates now in the direst peril, but they could do nothing about it as the German ship carried on to port.

Through that Sunday those five men huddled on the *Ann* with the rising tide sending waves crashing down on it. Two men were so disturbed by the fearsome spectacle of these roaring waves that they climbed into the shrouds and lashed themselves there for the night. At about nine o'clock on Monday morning the *Ann* was spotted by a passing fishing smack which was able to negotiate the shallows. Its crew found that the men who had lashed themselves into the shrouds were already dead from exposure. The other three men were on the point of death, having given up hope of rescue.

This awful shipwreck 250 years ago was the outcome of a very ordinary trading voyage undertaken by hundreds of ships up and down our coast every day. The risk was always there, the haunting thought behind every weighing of the anchor, every casting off from the quay. It surely says something for the courage and character of the sailors in the merchant fleets of those days.

Never A Shot In Anger

The *Colchester* was a 4th Rate fighting ship of 976 tons mounting 50 guns, built for the Navy at the Harwich yard early in 1744. For all its stout timbers, its forest of masts and spars, its suits of sails, it did not last one year.

Not long after it was launched, the *Colchester* went aground on the edge of that perilous passage, the Knock Deep, between the sandbanks of the Kentish Knock and the Long Sand. Did the officer on watch give the wrong command to the helmsman? Was there some sudden, overpowering storm? We shall never know now. However, it developed a leak, before or after the grounding, which was so bad that the unfortunate captain had to order the scuttling of this brand new ship there on the shallows, so that it would not lift off with the flowing tide into deep water where the chance of survival for the crew, many of whom could not swim, would be negligible.

Then he had to give a signal of his distress to other warships which might be in the vicinity. This he did by firing the guns, singly, at intervals. One hundred and forty explosions heard by people along the coast of Essex and Kent caused rumours to fly around that there was a big battle going on out at sea, for England and France had been at war since 1739 in the dispute known as the War of Jenkin's Ear. No battleship or merchantman heaved over the horizon in response to this long, loud call for help. A warship at the Nore, the old gathering place for the fleet in

A ship of the Colchester class as it appears in a painting by Willem Van de Velde.

the Thames estuary opposite Sheerness, did hear that signal and interpreted it correctly as that of a sister-ship in deep distress, but the wind was blowing from quite the wrong quarter for it to get out to the Kentish Knock. It answered with a cannonade from its own guns – and hoped for a timely change of wind.

18

The captain of the *Colchester* could not wait for help. He had a crew of more than 400 men to be saved from the sea. It was necessary to get a boat back to the nearest port, Harwich, and lead rescuers out to the Knock Deep. He ordered the longboat to be lowered and manned by 13 men to put plenty of muscle behind the oars. It was upset by the heavy seas and not a man was saved. Another boat was hoisted out and lowered away. It survived the launching, breasted the waves, disappeared over the horizon.

Then followed an agonizing wait on the upper deck as the sinking ship settled deeper and deeper into the sand. Hour followed hour, the tide gurgled ever higher through the lower decks, then receded reluctantly, like a lion deprived of its prey. At last a look-out high in the rigging reported a speck on the horizon. The speck became a sail and, one by one, six separate small boats hove into view. The *Colchester*'s boat had made it to port and brought back five Harwich smacks. They crammed them as full as they dared with the shipwrecked sailors and, coming and going through the day, they brought 365 men safely back to Harwich. Sad to say, in the haste and confusion of the stranding and the scuttling, 16 sick sailors deep in the bowels of the ship were drowned before they could be rescued. Including them and the longboat's crew and other accidents, a total of 41 men were lost.

To the best of my knowledge the *Colchester* was too deep in the sand and too far from shore facilities to be recovered. It had been built and wrecked within a year and all its 50 cannon lie like fossil creatures enveloped in the dreaded sands of the Kentish Knock.

Hoisting The Captain Aloft

On the evening of Thursday 8th December 1815 the landlubbers locking their doors and closing their shutters felt the rising wind and saw it catch their candles, setting them a-fluttering. Anyone who lived along the coast would have given a thought to the sailors out there on the sea in the blackness of the night. As they kneeled to say their prayers beside a warm, inviting bed they would have included a plea for the safety of those men who endured such hardship to bring them the necessities and the luxuries of life.

That it was a bad night was proved to them by the report in their newspaper a week later: 'The damage done to the shipping on this coast in the late gales has been immense. A great number of vessels of various descriptions have arrived at Harwich, with the loss of anchors, cables, masts, &c.' Those vessels, and their crews were lucky – they got into port. The brig *Palemon* did not. It had sailed successfully all the way from Zante, one of the Ionian Isles off Greece in the Mediterranean and was making its way up the coast of East Anglia to Blythe with nothing more than a luxury – a cargo of currants.

How it came so close to the shore is not known. It may have been the constant tacking against a stiff nor'easter which brought it into the shallows over Andrews Shoal, somewhere between Landguard Point and Felixstowe. It struck bottom and with a falling tide, that boded ill.

Where the sea met the outfall of the Orwell and the Stour rivers there was a maelstrom so whipped up by the wind that, though their plight had been seen from the shore there was no boat of any kind which dared to run the gauntlet to their rescue. The *Palemon* settled in the sands, the seas broke over her, the crew had to take to the rigging as the tide swept in.

The captain had already broken his leg in a fall whilst fighting the gale the day before. Now, when the tide came in, the crew had to hoist him in a sling up to the 'tops' – the rigging above the mainsail, where he hung out of harm's way until the ebbing tide allowed him to be lowered down on deck again. This was a bitter December's day and they were without any means of obtaining food.

A number of un-named heroes on shore could stand by no longer. They set out in a boat to force their way through the waves. Their boat was swamped before they made it, and it was only with the greatest difficulty that they were able to clamber aboard the brig. Now, with no way back, they were in the same perilous position as the crew they were trying to save.

Thankfully the storm abated during the night and next morning other seamen from the shore made another determined effort, reached the wreck and brought everybody safely off. The paper reported the happy ending in the rolling language of the day: 'The Captain is extremely ill. The crew, by cautious and humane treatment, are likely to do well. Great Praise is due to those men who, at the hazard of their own lives, endeavoured to rescue their fellow men from perishing, and at last so happily succeeded.'

All For The Want
Of An Anchor

The traffic on the highway of the sea up the East Anglian coast 200 years ago can be likened to the lorries which throng our motorways today. Just as drivers recount how bad luck and mechanical failures led to their accidents, so the seaman from a coaster back in 1818 could tell his story of misfortune and death which all began with a broken link in an anchor chain.

The *Speedwell* was a brigantine – a two-masted ship, square-rigged on the foremast and fore-and-aft rigged on the mainmast. This was a type of ship favoured by brigands and pirates because it was not too big, was easily managed under sail and had a good turn of speed, and thus the type became named after them. This small ship swims out of history in the pages of the *Colchester Gazette* on 21st March 1818 where it is reported: 'Amongst the numerous melancholy incidents which occurred on the coast during the late tremendous storm we have to relate the following: the *Speedwell*, brigantine of Ipswich bound to Sunderland for coals, in ballast, struck off Souter Point.'

Now Souter Point is not a feature of East Anglia, it is a headland some three miles north of Sunderland, divided from it by Whitburn Bay; but in every other respect the connection is definitely with Suffolk – the ship's home port, its captain and his family, their home at Somersham,

The brigantine was one of the smallest type of sailing ships carrying square rig on the foremast only. The brigantine *Speedwell's* fate was sealed when its anchor broke while riding out a gale.

and even the destination of the cargo it was going to collect – so it merits inclusion in this book.

This trading ship was the pride of its owner and captain, John Brown of Somersham, a village northwest of Ipswich. He obviously was not expecting trouble on this trip from Ipswich, for he had taken his third daughter Mary along, together with two sons, John and Robert, who helped to work the ship. The rest of the crew consisted of four men and a cabin boy. When the storm began to blow the captain took every precaution. He reduced sail to the barest minimum needed to keep the *Speedwell* under control and hove to with his anchor out. That is when the misfortune began.

Being unladen, the brigantine was high out of the water, like a huge sail to the wind. The gale blew so hard that the ship strained at its anchor. A pin broke, or the cable

23

parted. It was impossible to see or say just what happened down there underwater. Freed from its restraint the *Speedwell* drifted rapidly away at the mercy of the wind and the current. It struck the shallows where the sands stretched out far from the shore. There was no point in everybody staying on board the stranded brigantine, risking their lives as the heavy seas smashed into it. John Brown thought it was best for everybody who could to get ashore whilst the tide was ebbing.

The longboat was hoisted over the side very quickly and all but two of the crew took their places in it. Those two unselfishly remained aboard the *Speedwell*. With hindsight that was as wise as it was unselfish. The captain, rightly concerned for his children's safety, saw that they were in the longboat.

Was there then a falling out; or did he consider the longboat was dangerously overloaded? We shall never know, but it seems that the captain was so confident that he could get to dry land up the long, gently sloping sands, although they were covered in places by the tide which had started sweeping in, that he ordered the coxswain of the longboat to land his daughter, his elder son, himself and one of the crew on a flat rock. He must have thought that he could wade ashore from there in greater safety than in staying in the overcrowded boat. He was also increasing the chances of survival of the rest of the crew and his other son by taking all that extra weight out of the boat.

The paper reports that the longboat then went on its way, to a more distant part of the rock where they succeeded in reaching the shore. The captain's group waded away, trying to beat the tide, swimming across channels where there were deep waters. Mary grew tired and then utterly exhausted, her father stayed to help her. The sea crept up and overwhelmed them. They drowned.

Only his son and the seaman made it to the shore and they were in a totally exhausted condition.

Back on the *Speedwell*, now firmly in the sand and being battered to pieces by the huge waves formed by the wind over the shallows, the two remaining members of the crew decided that their only possible avenue of escape was to head for the shore as fast as they could. Through the rising tide they stumbled and swam their way to safety.

How sad it was for John Brown's widow. She lost her husband, her daughter and the ship – the means of the family's livelihood. She would have been shown sympathy, but in those hard days such suffering was too common to be the cause of much fuss. In fact, in that family alone seven other men had been drowned or otherwise killed in similar separate incidents.

The Mighty *Marquis*

We can contrast the personal tragedy of the loss of a small ship and the death of its owner-captain with the fate that same year of a great ship heading for London from the other side of the world. The *Marquis of Wellington* was an East Indiaman – one of the grandest sights to be seen when, in light winds, it moved majestically and apparently effortlessly through sparkling seas with all sails set, 28 of them on three masts tall as a steeple and a long jib-boom pointing way out ahead of the bows.

She was of 653 tons burthen, built at Calcutta for the East India Company in 1801. Her scantling, or timber-work, used timbers of teak, of larger and stronger dimensions than usual. Other Indian woods, then considered rare and costly, were used in the superstructure. The *Marquis of Wellington* showed its up-to-dateness in the copper-sheathing of its bottom, to defeat the fouling and the rotting which so affected wooden ships. On its sides, from the deepest-laden watermark down to the sheathing, copper nails were used because they resisted corrosion from salt water so much better than iron. So this was a well-found ship with many years of useful service before it.

The grand ship had once again come home from India with a vast cargo of cotton, cotton yarn, ginger, indigo, sugar, rice and all sorts of exotic novelties. It was practically in the mouth of the Thames when it struck bottom on the Mouse, a sandbank ten miles east of Shoeburyness.

That dreaded trap for the unwary has been called the Mouse for more than 400 years, and now nobody knows why. The crew and passengers were quickly rescued without injury, but getting such a great ship off the sand was quite another matter.

Whilst the owners and the insurers were discussing the problem and negotiating over the loss there was many an Essex smack, and not a few from Kent as well, which chose a moonlit night and a quiet sea to do a little salvage on their own behalf. These self-employed 'salvagers' were hardly more than looters in the way they stripped all the running rigging, ropes, anchors, and all the other equipment they could free from its fixings. They hardly had to take it ashore to dispose of it, for there were dozens of ships passing daily up and down this main sea road from London to Scotland and many of their masters were ready to bargain for all kinds of useful odds and ends. When the smacks were seen to be coming ashore with bag after bag of rice and sugar however, the authorities had to act. Through the office of the Essex Vice-Admiralty an advertisement was inserted in the *Colchester Gazette* of 21st March 1818:

'Whereas the East India Ship *Marquis of Wellington* was lately WRECKED upon the Mouse Sand, and a great part of her Cargo, consisting of Cotton, Cotton Yarn, Ginger, Indigo, Sugar, Rice and other articles, have been taken from the Wreck, and fraudulently concealed and disposed of; THIS IS TO GIVE NOTICE, That any PERSON RECEIVING, BUYING, or HAVING in their POSSESSION any part of the said Ship's Cargo, will be guilty of FELONY. And all Salvors, Boatmen, Hovellors [unlicensed salvagers], and others, finding or having Possession of any part of the said SHIP'S STORES, MATERIALS, or CARGO, are hereby CAUTIONED to duly report the same at this Office, or to Some of my Admiralty

27

Agents, agreeable to Act of Parliament, as In the event of their not doing so, they will be prosecuted with the utmost vigour of the Law.'

An official warning was not likely to deter the Essex 'salvagers'. Ten miles away from the nearest Admiralty Office, out amongst the wind and the waves, where the smacksmen made the rules, the *Marquis of Wellington* lay like a honeypot swarming with bees. Nevertheless some of these salvagers were properly employed to bring ashore as much as they could. Within a fortnight advertisements appeared offering, 'About 500 bushels of PEARL RICE, part of the cargo of the East India Ship *Marquis of Wellington*, which is now completely dry and fit for use. It is well worth the attention of Families, having been found most excellent for puddings, bread, &c and will be sold at ... 1½d per Pound.' Colchester auctioneers were also offering six tons of sugar, one ton of ginger and 'a quantity of Munject' which had already been brought out of the ship.

The illegal salvaging continued all through the summer and autumn on such a scale that the Essex Vice-Admiralty Office was moved to advertise once again the awful penalties which awaited those who were still picking over the wreck when tide and weather were favourable. Rewards of £10 and £20 were offered for information about and apprehension of 'any Smack or Vessel which may have picked up any Anchor, Cable, Wreckage, Goods, Merchandize, or Ships' Stores ...'. The ship itself was never recovered. It was sold off as it lay there on the Mouse, to offset the underwriters' loss. It would have been a bargain for a lively London dealer – if only he could have kept those Essex smacksmen at bay!

Pluck and Plunder

Shipwreck can bring out the best and the worst in folk. Strangely enough the two extremes are clearly illustrated by the stories of two ships wrecked by the same savage storm – on 24th February 1837.

Let us take the story of pluck first, and set the scene. It was a Friday when the storm blew up to its height. The wind was raging out of the north, flinging sleet and rain like bullets at the boiling sea. Ships ran for shelter. Too far out to reach the safe haven of a port they crowded into the Swin, the deep channel well off the coast of the Dengie Peninsula of Essex, where they could shelter between the sandbanks of the Gunfleet and East Barrow. Even here though, the wind blew so hard that several ships broke their anchor chains and went aground. One ship wrecked on the Heaps sand at the height of the storm could not be identified – all its crew were drowned and the vessel pounded into such pieces that its name was never found.

Two colliers sailing with others in a kind of convoy for company, could be identified and were helped. They were both on their way from North Shields to London but had run for shelter to the Swin. The *St Lawrence*, blown on the sands behind the Middle Swin at ten o'clock at night, broke up very quickly. Salvage smacks were there to lend the crew a hand. They could not save the coal but they did recover most of the ship's stores which were landed, with the crew, at Wivenhoe on the following day. The other collier was the *John Hunter* of 260 tons burthen. It was blown on to the sands nearby. Pounded by the breakers it was badly holed. When the tide rose it floated off and was once again anchored in the Swin channel. By now, though, it was taking so much water that the pumps could not cope with it.

To prevent it sinking in this deep water, where nothing could be saved, the master ordered the anchor cable to be dropped overboard, then he had all the sails set that could be and so ran the *John Hunter* well and truly ashore on the East Barrow sands. In lowering their longboat and rowing it through the wild waves in this manoeuvre one man was lost when he was flung out of the boat by a massive breaker. He left a wife and three children back home in North Shields, but his mates were not in any position to search for him.

They got the vessel on the sands but it did not settle sufficiently to keep it upright as the tide receded. It heeled over more and more in the shallower water until the eight remaining crew were forced to climb out into the, by now, cantilevered main-topmast crosstrees, where they could only cling to the rigging and hope for help. For a day and a night and into the next day they clung there. Then, with the wind abating, two Brightlingsea salvage smacks made the risky journey to their aid. They were the *Elizabeth and Ann* and the *Robert* sailed by Joseph Pennick and Robert Tracey respectively. They found the shipwrecked sailors in a serious plight. They had neither eaten nor drunk for 30 hours, and for most of that time their legs had been dangling in that stormy, wintry sea. The smacksmen got them all into their boats and landed them safely at Brightlingsea.

The newspaper reporting the shipwreck concluded; 'Too much praise cannot be bestowed towards those, who, at the hazard of their own lives, rescued those of their fellow creatures.' The rescued men were so grateful that when they got back to North Shields, they took the unusual step of writing a letter of thanks, signed, or marked by those who could not write, by Richard Long, the master, John Kell, the mate, John Sanderson, Thomas Foster, Andrew Muir and James Halcrow and last but not least the two 'boys' Henry Scott and Samuel Barber. It runs:

'We the undersigned, being the master, mate and survivors of the snow *John Hunter* of the port of North Shields, which vessel is now a wreck on the East Barrows Sand, off this coast, consider it our duty to return heartfelt and grateful acknowledgements to Mr Joseph Pennick and the crew of the smack *Elizabeth and Ann*, and to Mr Robert Tracey and the crew of the smack *Robert*, for their prompt and zealous exertions in saving ourselves from the wreck, after having been exposed for 26 hours during a heavy gale of wind, and compelled for safety to cling to the main-topmast crosstrees, the whole time expecting the mast to give way, the vessel having fallen over on her side, and the lower and topsail yards being under water.

'In the performance of this arduous service the parties were compelled to run their vessels into danger; and at the risk of their own lives, came with their boats through the breakers and the heavy sea on the sand, evincing in the hour of peril, the greatest degree of judgment and humanity, and after having got us safely on board the smack *Elizabeth and Ann* every attention was paid that our destitute condition required, until we arrived in safety at Brightlingsea on Saturday evening, the 25th of February.'

It was on that same day, 24th February 1837, that the *Raby Castle*, about 160 tons, master's name Greensides, was proceeding from London to its home port of Stockton with a crew of seven, two passengers and a very valuable cargo. The storm was beyond anything the crew had ever experienced. There was nothing they could do; the ship was blown by the wind from the north, northwest until it ran aground on the long, long sandy shore of Cley-next-the-Sea. The captain kept his head and got the longboat launched. Everybody crowded into it and ran the gauntlet of the roaring breakers to come at last to dry land.

When the tide had receded it could be seen that the *Raby Castle* was hard aground in shallow water. At the turn of the tide the storm-tossed sea battered it continually, breaking it up and washing out the cargo. By half-flood that cargo was truly translated into flotsam, washed ashore in a wide band up the almost flat sand when the tide turned again. The news soon got round. As early as seven in the morning some 300 people were there on the beach watching the *Raby Castle* break up. Within the hour the crowd had doubled, with rich pickings in minds.

The paper of the day reports: '. . . immediately after she broke up the beach was strewed with spirits, wine, oranges, nuts, teas, toys, hampers, boxes, etc, etc and a scene which beggars description ensued. The numbers [of people] continued to increase till noon, during which time the most outrageous and beastly conduct was exhibited – here might be observed a group broaching a spirit cask and letting it run into their oilskin hats, shoes etc, there another set filling their pockets and handkerchiefs, further on another party secreting a cask, etc, until a more favourable opportunity presented itself of disposing of it, and all this in the face of day and in a civilised country – plunder, wholesale plunder appeared to be the order of the day in spite of agents, coastguard men, etc.'

Lieutenant George Howes RN, the coastguard officer and the men under his command were there alright, but they found it impossible to police such a long stretch of the coast where the goods were coming ashore. He had a further problem in that many of the men he had told off to guard collections of goods succumbed to temptation, took a drink of those spirits, and then themselves went on a looting spree. Quite a few people, men and women, drank so much on the spot that they had to be carried off dead drunk. Sadly then this storm was remembered for plunder as much as for pluck. The cargo of the *Raby Castle* had been worth £5,000 – only about £800 worth was ever recovered. The remains of the ship, easily recoverable at low tide in good weather, sold at auction for just £41.

Steam-paddle-tug towing the lifeboat out. From George Mears's painting *To The Rescue.*

Spanish Salvage

From the spelling of its name you can guess that the *Independiente* was Spanish. It had a long journey ahead of it when it cleared Hamburg, for it was heading for Havana. But, sad to say, it did not even get out of the North Sea. On a stormy day in March 1842, it drove aground on the West Rocks due east of Walton-on-the-Naze. By then the ship was so far off course that the mate told his rescuers that he reckoned they were off South Foreland and that they had hit the Goodwin Sands east of Ramsgate.

It was the Essex smacksmen-salvagers who saw the ship's distress. They set off to save the crew and claim the salvage if they could. The rescue fleet was made up of the *Friends Goodwill* under S. Wisbey and the steamer *Brocklebank* from Colchester, and *Celerity* under J. Manning and *Aurora's Increase* under William Lewis, both from Harwich. With their shallower draught they could easily get alongside the big ship. Their experience on this coast and their superb seamanship made it look easy.

The Spanish captain was only too pleased to place his ship and crew in their capable hands. Wisbey took over, sized up the situation, and by an astute setting of the sails got the *Independiente* off the sands and into the channel called The Gullet, where it floated freely, though the rudder had to be unshipped and hoisted clear so that it would not foul the bottom and put a strain on the stern frame. William Lewis, one of a famous family of Harwich salvagers, then came into the picture.

He wanted to try a trick by which the little smack could nudge the big *Independiente* along the channels through the sands those smacksmen knew so well. He set the Spanish ship's sails to give a slow forward movement, then, lashing his smack to the stern on the windward side he trimmed his own sails to act as a rudder in keeping the *Independiente* on the intended course. As it turned out the *Aurora's Increase* could not exercise sufficient control to beat against the strong wind out of the north; they had to settle for a way through the Wallet, where the Revenue Cutter *Desmond*, commanded by Isaac Saxby, broke off its anti-smuggling patrol to give a hand in bringing the *Independiente* to a sheltered anchorage in the Colne. But such are the vagaries of our climate that the wind dropped and they could not keep enough momentum to ensure a safe passage through the lines of craft already at anchor.

So rescued and rescuers found a safe anchorage, the Revenue Cutter sailed away on its own business and Lewis took his smack into Brightlingsea to summon further aid. He cadged a lift on a cart to Colchester where he headed for his old friends on the *Brocklebank*, formerly a steam packet on the Colchester to London run. Now it acted as a tug, but the crew had to be dug out of a pub, and there was a good deal of haggling over the price before they agreed to get up steam and make the short trip down the Colne. They finally agreed on a fee of £25, with £5 to be refunded to the smacksmen if they also got the job of towing the *Independiente* round to Harwich for inspection and repair. All went well. Thankfully there had been no loss of life and the Spaniards pass out of the story.

But the smacksmen had to wait for their reward, and, let us remember, the cost of their part in the rescue, for the *Aurora's Increase* had lost her own ship's boat during all these manoeuvres, until their salvage claim came up in court. Counsel for the smacksmen valued the cargo they had saved at £20,000 and pointed out that if they had not gone out to save the crew and the ship but left it to break up and then recovered the cargo they would have been allowed one third of the value. To the surprise of all the seafaring men in court the award was only £450. The smacksmen were so angry that they threatened to appeal to the Admiralty Court. Since that would have meant further delay and argument the owners of the *Indepen-diente* offered an extra £100. The smacksmen reluctantly accepted – and went straight back to sea. Courts were not for the likes of them. The sea they could understand – and respect.

Victim of the Gunfleet

The dreaded Gunfleet sandbank is not a modern manifestation of coastal erosion. It is named in official documents as early as 1320, long before the days of printing, where it is shown as 'Gunfletsond'. It takes its name from the Gan Fleet, the old name for the Holland Brook which divided Great Holland and Little Holland, now part of Clacton, and ran out into the Wallet Channel. This sandbank and those running parallel with it seawards – East Barrow, Sunk Sand, Long Sand and Kentish Knock, make a maze of danger which confused so many mariners. The flat shoreline on either side of the Channel was a further complication, leading sailors to think they were off the French coast when they were in amongst the sandbanks, or that they were well out in the Channel when they were in fact heading into the Thames estuary.

The lighthouse which guided vessels off the Gunfleet was not built until 1852. Thirty years before this, 14 ships were blown on the Gunfleet in one gale. The amazing thing is that on this occasion not a life was lost and all but two of the ships were subsequently refloated. Even while the lighthouse was being built two ships, lost in the blackness of the night, blundered on the sand. The building contractors were able to use their tug to get one of the ships off again – and claim the salvage!

A good example of the terrible conditions in which the crew of a stricken ship could find themselves is that of the brig *Traveller*. It had completed most of its voyage from Hartlepool to London when a terrible gale blew up on the night of Saturday, 17th February 1843. Despite all their efforts the crew could not prevent it being blown ashore on the Gunfleet. Those ten men went through the night feeling the brig literally breaking up under their feet. In the early morning light the wreck was sighted by two Colchester smacks, the *New Gipsy* and the *Atalanta*. They could see from afar the *Traveller* hard in the grip of the sand, with waves breaking right over her and black blobs in the rigging which they knew were men in their last throes, washed by the waves and battered by a freezing February gale.

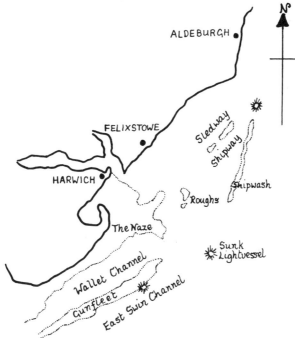

Sketch map showing the treacherous Gunfleet sandbank, where the brigantine *Traveller* came to grief in 1843.

All that Sunday the smacks could only stand by help-lessly as the waves flung up by the storm over the shallows pounded the wreck and made any attempt at rescue doomed to failure and the loss of life. The smacksmen's situation was already dangerous as they pitched and tossed just off the sands, waiting and hoping for the chance to move in and help. They hoisted their colours, the only signal they could think of which would show the *Traveller* that they would keep standing by. Men in the rigging let go with one hand to show with a wave that they understood and appreciated the message. Through the day and on through Sunday night the smacks swung to their anchors, watching the weather; expecting that in the night some of the *Traveller*'s crew must surely have been overcome by exhaustion and despair and dropped into that raging sea. On Monday morning the smacksmen anxiously counted those tiny figures again – they were all there!

Knowing that they could not hold on for much longer, and despite the unabated violence of the sea, the smacks-men launched their two small boats and pulled through the white water to the wreck. In the words of the local newspaper for that week, '. . . as they entered the breakers all found it to be the most fearful position in which they were ever placed; but after being buffeted for a consider-able time, they at length succeeded in reaching the wreck, and took from the rigging the whole crew, ten in number, six in the *New Gipsy*'s boat and four in the *Atalanta*'s.'

With all these extra men aboard and the strength of the wind, they could not risk the same route back to their smacks. They could not agree on which was the wisest course so they went their separate ways, one to the lee-ward of the wreck and the other into the Swin channel where, most fortunately, it was sighted by the steamship *Gazelle* on its way from London to Hull. The *Gazelle* lay to, took on the six men from the *New Gipsy* and waited

40

for the *Atalanta* to come up with the other four men. On the way, the rescued men had been given refreshment. Their clothes had had to be cut off because their limbs were too swollen from exposure for the smacksmen to get them off any other way. In a final gesture of generosity, the smacksmen gave some of their own clothes to the survivors before they transferred them to the *Gazelle*.

The 'Wicked Wrecks'

The Scroper's son, that old sea dog of a character in the late Hervey Benham's *The Salvagers* was a forthright fellow – 'Some of the most wicked wrecks was the old emigrant ships, time they were shipping thousands of Germans out to the colonies. They crammed them aboard of ships that hadn't got no idea how to find their way out of the North Sea.' The *Johann Frederick* was a case in point, though there is no evidence to suggest that it was not well found and seaworthy.

As far as the newspapers were concerned the story broke on Saturday, 25th October 1850, at about two o'clock, when the smack *Eagle*, under Captain Easter, tied up at the Wivenhoe quay and put ashore 40 or so survivors, including the captain and mate of a vessel wrecked on the Gunfleet sands, which run parallel with the coast from the Naze down to the Colne estuary. They were from the *Johann Frederick*, 305 tons burthen, commanded by Captain Whieting, bound from Bremen to Charleston, South Carolina, with some 160 hopeful emigrants, mostly female, looking forward to all the opportunities offered by life in the New World.

When the ship set sail on Monday 21st October the weather was favourable enough, but a combination of thick haze and an increasingly boisterous wind made it impossible for the captain to take astronomical observations and get a 'fix'. By Thursday he reckoned they were running down the French coast. Nobody could have been more surprised when, at ten that night, a terrible judder and a sickening lurch told him that the *Johann Frederick* had gone aground, on the Gunfleet as he was later to learn from his rescuers. At this time most of the passengers were already tucked up in bed. The shock brought them tumbling out, literally and metaphorically, to find out what had happened. They were close to panic. The blackness of the night and the grinding of the vessel on the sand in heavy seas caused consternation in the crew as well. With each bump upon the sandbank the ship seemed to settle deeper.

The captain kept a clear head however and ordered the standard blue lights and other indications of distress to be burnt. No ship answered the call. The captain, fearing the vessel, now well on the sands, might fall over broadside on, set the crew to cutting away most of the spars to prevent it becoming top-heavy. When Friday dawned flags were hoisted on each of the masts as further distress signals. Smacksmen from Wivenhoe and Harwich, out early for their fishing, saw these signals and hastened to the rescue. With the *Eagle*, already mentioned, went *Louisa*, *Benevolence*, *Mary* and *Elizabeth*, all from Wivenhoe, with others from Harwich whose names went unrecorded. Anchoring off the dreaded Gunfleet sands, they manned their small boats and rowed through the huge breakers, truly risking their own lives to get alongside the ill-fated *Johann Frederick*.

Once they got aboard the wreck the smacksmen helped the unfortunate emigrants into their boats for transfer to the smacks. Many of the smacksmen stayed on the wreck to make more room in the boats for the shipwrecked. So half of them were brought off to safety before the flooding tide and a rising wind made a further journey to the wreck quite impossible. Until the tide turned and the sea moderated some hundred or more men and women were trapped on the wreck. It gave signs of heeling over, with the sea constantly scouring its decks. Smacksmen and crew worked hard in terrible conditions to cut away the main-mast and to secure ropes across the decks for the passengers still left aboard to hold on to, otherwise they might have been washed overboard. This is exactly what happen-ed to some trunks and other baggage which had been brought up on deck ready for the smacksmen's next journey.

By this time the sea had filled the vessel to such a degree that it was in danger of breaking up completely and taking with it all those remaining on board. But the smacksmen knew their stuff. The turn of the tide brought a calmer sea; even then it was so rough that the little boats could have been smashed against the wreck. So they anchored off the Sands, passed ropes through the shallow, broken water and so hauled everyone on board the *Johann Frederick* to safety on the smacks. The captain, who, it was reported, had behaved admirably throughout, was the last to leave his ship.

The ordeal for those poor would-be emigrants was not over. They still had to undergo a thoroughly uncomfort-able voyage of some 20 miles to Harwich during Friday and Saturday with absolutely nothing but the sodden clothes in which they sat in the overcrowded smacks. A few of the emigrants, some 40 or so, went with the Wivenhoe smacks to that port. They arrived hungry, wet, cold and mentally and physically worn out, but Lloyd's agent there, Mr J. G. Chamberlain soon had them settled in the Rose and Crown and other temporary lodgings. On the Monday they were taken to London at the expense of the Eastern Counties Railway and placed in the care of the Bremen consul. The Harwich party met them there after being brought down by sea on the steamer *Adonis*.

The ship became a total wreck, the general cargo valued at 2,000 dollars was lost, but thankfully every one of those emigrants and the crew was saved!

Looting on the Middle Swin

Poor Captain John Skelton, his troubles began on Wednesday 13th November in 1861. From Whitby he had taken his brig *Regina* all the way to Cronstadt in Russia, near Leningrad, to pick up a cargo of tallow and lathwood. That was a difficult journey in harsh winter weather, but all had gone well and he was looking forward to his arrival in London the following day when he felt the dreaded shudder and saw the bellying of the sails which told him and his crew that they were aground on the Middle Swin Sands, just below the lightship and some eight miles out from the estuary of the river Crouch. The crew became so fearful that they immediately lowered the longboat and told the captain that if he and his wife did not get a move on they would go without them. Since the *Regina* was already showing signs of breaking up the captain, out of consideration for his wife's safety, had to hurry her into the boat without being able to take any of the ship's documents and instruments with him.

The storm was so severe that they could not sail the boat to the coast so they were very fortunate that the schooner *Effort* saw their plight and took them on to its destination at Whitstable, 18 miles due south. As soon as they arrived the following morning Captain Skelton signalled for a smack to come out to the *Effort* where it lay at anchor.

Two came, so he hired them both to take his mate Thomas Coates to stand by the wreck until he could get further instructions as to recovery of ship and cargo, as well as arrangements for the accommodation of the crew ashore.

He was not able to get off the *Effort* to report the loss by telegraph until nine at night. Early on Friday afternoon he was at last free to hire another smack and set off back for the wreck. By the time he got there though, about six in the evening, it was already dark. He could discern a whole lot of boats tied up alongside the *Regina*, which was lying on its side in a much calmer sea. What is more he found the ship itself swarming with men like bees in a hive. These were the smacksmen salvagers from Brightlingsea. It had not taken long for them to hear there was an abandoned ship out there on the Middle Swin.

These cheeky sea scavengers had cut holes in the side of the brig to drag out casks of tallow. They had broken them open and were digging out the tallow with boathooks and their bare hands. Skelton hailed them, said he was the captain of the *Regina* and ordered them to leave, adding that he was having the wreck officially surveyed the next day. They told him they had found it as a deserted wreck and were within their rights. As it was, a strong breeze sprang up and they all had to leave the wreck for their own safety. The captain left the mate in the Whitstable smack to keep an eye on the *Regina* while he went back for rest and refreshment. But he was back at the wreck between three and four next morning.

Dawn would not illuminate the scene for hours, yet Captain Skelton saw so many boats tethered around the wreck that he could not get within four boats' lengths of it. The captain now had the Lloyd's agent with him and with that authority he told the men to leave at once. They told him they had as much right there as he did. The mate reported to him how he had seen the men forcing their

The brig was the work-horse of the coastal trade in the first half of the 19th century. Those unfortunate enough to founder became prey to the salvagemen who raced the authorities to the wreck for its cargo.

crowbars between the ship's timbers; he had remonstrated with them and they replied by pelting him with tallow and saying that they would just as soon put an axe into him as into the ship.

But Lloyd's knew their business; they had arranged for a special agent, Captain Russell, to take a steam tug out to the *Regina* to size up the situation, to take the *Regina* in tow if possible, or to recover the cargo. The tug could not stop the scavengers, but it could get down to Sheerness Dockyard and be back in the afternoon with a detachment of a dozen marines. The men were still crowded all round the wreck, with at least 25 smacks in attendance and their boats made fast to the *Regina* like beads on a necklace. Captain Skelton took the tug's boat to the wreck, cautioned the men again and only got insults for his pains so back he went to the tug and had the marines accompany him to the *Regina*. Now the scavengers could see that he meant business.

William Dove of the *Prima Donna*, which was already heavily laden with tallow, had told his crew to heave the anchor. Skelton told them to desist until the smack could be searched. Even with the backing of the marines, the smacksmen would not obey the order until the sergeant actually drew his bayonet. Skelton saw at once the vast amount of tallow they had taken so he ordered the master to go straight to Sheerness, and put two marines aboard to see that he was obeyed. This was going to be inconvenient to the smack's crew because they had come out from Brightlingsea. He caught the *Sarah* as well and gave its master the same orders. By this time the rest of the smacks were under weigh and heading for the coast with all speed, except for the *Spray*, but since it had only an insignificant amount of tallow on board it was allowed to follow the others.

In the fine weather that followed the tug was able to recover most of the remaining cargo, but the *Regina* was what we would call today 'a total write-off'.

The last chapter of the story takes place in court where James Gould, George Oliver, Charles Cook, William Dove, William Rumble, James Bacon and James Fielding of the smacks *Prima Donna* and *Sarah* were charged with feloniously carrying away a large quantity of tallow from the wreck of the brig *Regina*. For the Underwriters' Salvage Association of Lloyd's it was said that the charge was of the greatest importance to the whole of the mercantile community because it involved the protection of cargoes of vessels wrecked on the coast. But Lloyd's were not vindictive – they simply wanted to make the point, publicly, that it was a serious and punishable offence. Counsel for the smacksmen said they '... belonged to a body of men who had rendered great aid on the coast. They went out in all weathers to afford assistance in saving life and property and had performed many courageous acts.' He claimed they had found this vessel abandoned, had taken possession of it and had exercised their best judgment in saving what they could of her cargo. The court was not moved by these blandishments, it fined each man £100 or six months in jail. The smacksmens' appeal against this sentence was dismissed, 'without the slightest hesitation' on Tuesday 31st December.

Lost on the Long Sand

'Wreck of a German immigrant ship. Loss of 50 lives.'
That was the headline in the *Essex County Standard* for
10th December 1875. The terrible tragedy had occurred
on Monday 6th December, but news did not travel so fast
in those days and the *Standard*'s first report had to be
supplemented the following week. At first it had been
thought that between 300 and 400 passengers had been on
board but later reports put the number at 123 with a crew
of 130. Only 155 passengers and crew were saved.

The *Deutschland*, 3,000 tons, was the pride of the
North German Lloyd's Atlantic fleet, one of its largest and
best-appointed ships. It left Bremen for New York on
Saturday 4th December, intending to call at Southampton
for more passengers and mail. The passengers, mostly
travelling steerage, were for the most part poor emigrants
to America, looking forward to a new life full of hope in
the land of opportunity. The voyage, under Captain Brickerstein, had not started well. Most of Saturday night was
spent at anchor near the Weser lightship because an
intense fog made navigation hazardous. The fog was
cleared by an easterly gale with driving snow which made
visibility almost as difficult.

The captain had two pilots on board, but neither was
familiar with the Essex coast and there was no reason why
they should be. One was a German pilot to get away from
Bremen and the other was an English pilot to assist with

the winding way round the Isle of Wight and up South-ampton Water. The first hard news of the shipwreck was triggered by an artilleryman at the Naval Barracks at Sheerness looking seaward at six in the morning after a night on guard duty. He saw a small boat, with its sail up, being beaten up the beach by angry waves. It was too dark to see if there was anyone on board but something was surely wrong. He raised the alarm, the guard was turned out and a party of men was sent down to the beach to investigate. They hauled the boat up the beach and found three men in it.

Two of them, only partly dressed, were dead and already turning black from the dreadful exposure to that freezing gale. In the stern a third man sat. He was close to death himself and could only speak very feebly, in broken English. When they got him into the warmth of the bar-racks and he had recovered a little he was able to tell them that he was the quartermaster of the *Deutschland*. That meant little enough to the army officers, but they became very concerned when the German blurted out his news of the shipwreck and the fate of more than 250 passengers and crew. He went on to tell them how the big ship, carrying also a large cargo of mails and general goods, had gone aground in a fearful snowstorm. Through the night, seas had washed clear across it and waves broke over them from all directions.

The captain had had lifebelts issued to passengers and crew; then, fearing the ship was about to break up he ordered this survivor, Quartermaster August Beck, to supervise the lowering of the lifeboats. Beck had prepared two for launching, and went down with the second boat as it was lowered from the davits. The conditions were impossible, both boats were capsized. Beck's boat was overturned twice. Only three people managed to climb back into it and then it was torn from the three-inch rope

The *Deutschland* carrying emigrants to America struck a sandbank off Harwich in December 1875. This tragedy led to the stationing of a lifeboat at Harwich a year later.

which kept it at the ship's side. Beck could not get it back to the ship. One of the two men with him was so badly wounded when the boat capsized that he died soon after. All the quartermaster could do was to set the sail and drift before the wind. They saw several ships but, because they were so low in the water, their distress signals were not noticed. The second man died and Beck was left alone to beach the boat guided by the light from the barracks.

Back on the *Deutschland* the captain postponed any further launching of the boats because of the extreme danger. They never did get launched because the heavy seas, sweeping the decks, stove them all in. Another survivor rounded out the story with the following statement: 'The steamer struck on Monday morning at five o'clock. The sea was very rough and it was blowing hard from the east-north-east, thick with snow. The lead was cast every half hour. We found 24 fathoms, then 17 fathoms. Immediately afterwards, going dead slow, she struck. The engines were turned full speed astern, and the ship straightway lost its propeller. The heavy seas drove the ship further up the sand . . . During Monday a lot of cargo from the forward hold was thrown overboard in an attempt to keep the ship's stern to the sea.' Pumps were kept going all day, with male passengers willingly taking their turn until darkness fell around four o'clock. Then the tide rose and passengers and crew had to take to the rigging, for the decks became awash. 'Capt Brickerstein remained on the bridge until he was washed out by the sea and had to join the others in the rigging.'

Back on shore at Harwich distress rockets had been seen rising up throughout the night and experienced seamen put the *Deutschland* as being aground on the Kentish Knock, the second outermost shifting shoal far out from the mouth of the Thames. The *Times* newspaper slated the town of Harwich for not having a lifeboat and criticised the seamen of that port for not getting together to go to the rescue of a ship in distress, even though they had fired an answering rocket to the ship's distress signals. But it should be said that those seamen would have had to row, and sail if the gale permitted, 27 miles out to the wreck. They knew well enough that they would not have survived the storm over that distance to be of help.

At five on Tuesday morning the steam tug *Liverpool* cast off from the quay at Harwich and made all speed to the *Deutschland*. She found the proud steamship was now a pitiful wreck, her decks entirely awash and breaking up, with survivors clinging to the rigging on that intensely cold December day. The tide was right for the tug to take off 120 people, including the captain and all but one of the officers. The reporter for the *Essex Standard* described the scene at the wreck on the arrival of the tug as '. . . beyond description. Strong men, women and children were clinging to the rigging as their only resource, some in their last struggles of death; and in the cabins could be seen the corpses of ladies as they had lain down calmly to rest, and poor children also.' On deck there was the horrifying spectacle of a headless body washing to and fro across the deck. It was the remains of a brave man. From his perch in the rigging he had seen a woman struggling across the deck, knocked down by the huge waves. He lashed a line to the rigging, tied it round his body and went to her rescue. But before he could reach her he was swept away by a wave so powerful that when he hit the bulwark his head was literally knocked off.

A final tally of people rescued came to 155, of whom 86 were crew. Of the passengers 48 were men and 21 were women and children. The tugmen even recovered 25 bags of mail which had been under water for almost a day. It was the appalling loss of life in this tragedy that led to the stationing of a lifeboat at Harwich in 1876. Called the *Springwell*, it was officially handed over to the town on the first anniversary of the wreck of the *Deutschland*.

The Death Throes of
The Indian Chief

The Long Sand justifies its name. It is a sandbank some 15 miles long running northeast from its wide base about 20 miles east of the Crouch estuary. Navigable channels divide it from the Sunk sand nearer the coast, and the Kentish Knock, the last hazard to be negotiated on the way to the open sea. A wreck on the Long Sand could be reached as directly from Ramsgate as it could from Harwich. The indentations of the Kent and Essex coasts, complicated by the convolutions of the Thames estuary, put other places at a disadvantage when rapid rescue was the order of the day.

There was, no doubt, a healthy rivalry amongst the lifeboat crews from stations round this coast in the race to the wreck and the saving of survivors. The wrecking of the *Indian Chief* illustrates this. She was a large vessel of 1,238 tons, fully loaded, and on her way from Middlesborough to Yokohama with a general cargo, having set out on the first day of the bright new year of 1881. Such a large ship, a barque which could set no less than 25 sails on its three masts and carried a pilot as well as the captain for this leg of the voyage, should have made the trip down the coast and into the Channel without much difficulty. When they picked up the beam from the lightship on the seaward side of the Knock Sand they were astonished to find they were

The steam-paddle-tug *Vulcan* towing the lifeboat *Bradford* from Ramsgate to go to the assistance of the *Indian Chief*. This barque grounded on Longsand in a gale on New Year's Day 1881.

on the wrong side of it. In the darkness and the rain of a windy, wintry night they were heading straight for the Long Sand. The wind had veered, was now blowing from the east, and so the *Indian Chief* was being driven closer and closer to the sandbank.

All the complicated manoeuvres were followed to turn the ship completely round and escape the trap. In trying to get it to 'come about', with the wheel put hard over, some elements of the rigging became entangled. Trying to sort it all out with the ship heeling over as it turned, and with the tops of the masts invisible in the darkness and the pouring rain, took so long that it could not save the ship. She grounded on the sands and began bumping horribly, lifted and dropped by the waves raised erratically by the wind and the tide over the shallow water. Nobody could be sent aloft to furl the sails because it felt as if the masts would be shaken out of the ship at any moment. All the sails had been released, to fly from the yards like flags in the wind.

The noise throughout those six hours before dawn was terrifying – the flapping and the whipcracking of the sails, the irregular thumping of the ship on the sand, and the furious beating of the waves in a roaring wind and hissing rain combined to make the mariners sure that their end had come. The captain acted responsibly enough. He had coloured rockets sent up as a distress signal to the light-ships, for ongoing transmission to the coast, and he had a big red flare lit and held high to catch the attention of any boat which might be in the vicinity. There was every hope that these signals would be seen in what was a very busy sea lane; and both the Knock and the Sunk lightships had sent up answering rockets.

Unbeknown to them a steamer, the *Nymphaea*, had grounded at the same time on the Sunk sand and had sent up distress rockets. So a whole chapter of mishaps ensued. The fishing smack *Albatross*, sailed by John Lewis, one of the famous Essex 'salvagers', saw the steamer's rockets and stood by her until daybreak. An attempt to get to her over the sands in those conditions would have been suici-dal. At daybreak Lewis also spotted the *Indian Chief* on the Long Sand. Luckily the smack *Aquiline* hove into view and was hailed for a quick conference on what to do next. The *Albatross* was to stand by as long as it could while the *Aquiline* crowded on all sail and raced to Harwich for the lifeboat. She went like a mad thing until the force of the wind sprung the boom from the mast. The *Aquiline* could then only limp into the Walton backwaters behind the Naze and well below Harwich. From here *Aquiline*'s mas-ter, Harry Cook walked eight miles or more from Oakley Creek to Harwich, getting there around eleven o'clock in the morning to alert the lifeboatmen.

To make headway out of the harbour against a dead east wind the lifeboat needed the help of a tug. They called on John Vaux, owner of the steam tug *Harwich*, which, with steam up already, was prepared for sea as quickly as was the lifeboat, the *Springwell*. The greatest delay was caused by the absence of three regular members of the crew, but by running round the town and shouting out the news, three replacements were found. By two o'clock the tug had towed the lifeboat clear out to the Sunk, where they saw the steamship *Nymphaea* stuck firmly in the sand with only funnel and masts showing above water. There was no sign of survivors.

There was nothing they could do there, so they carried on to look for the *Indian Chief*. They were still the wrong side of the Knock when they spotted her. With heavy seas drastically reducing the speed at which the *Harwich* could tow the *Springwell*, and with the early January twilight already upon them they were in a risky situation. Look at it from the tugman's view; John Vaux's tug was his living, his vital asset. He decided the risk involved was too great, ordered the tug to go about and head for Harwich. Without the tug the lifeboat could do nothing. It had to come back under tow, reaching Harwich around five p.m.

The benighted crew of the *Indian Chief* had now been marooned for over 14 hours and the rising tide brought waves sweeping across the deck. The Harwich lifeboatmen knew from experience what these poor men were enduring and they desperately wanted to get out there and do all they could to rescue them. They thought up the idea of getting a tow halfway or more by hitching up to the *Pacific* steam packet on its routine trip from Harwich to Antwerp at 9.30 p.m. They approached the Marine Superintendent of the Great Eastern Railway Company, who operated the ferry service, and, to their delight, he agreed.

The news got around the town and quite a crowd gathered to see their heroes off on their difficult voyage. The *Pacific* had to keep up a good speed to maintain control in the heavy seas and the wind which hit it head-on. This meant that the little lifeboat was being pulled clear through the waves. In no time at all it had filled, and under the added weight the tow-rope parted. The lifeboat seemed to shake itself like a dog, shed all its water and rose on the crests of the waves. The *Pacific* could not risk a turn to take up the tow again. It signalled its regret and steamed away on course. With great and tiring effort the lifeboat men turned the *Springwell* round, baled her out, and sailed her back to Harwich by midnight.

They were engaged next day in other rescues nearer at hand, so they were pleased to hear that another lifeboat, the *George Hounsfield* from Aldeburgh had been called out to the *Indian Chief*. Its news, when it returned that evening, was not so good. They had got out to the barque in improving weather but had found no sign of life aboard. This news was supplemented by a report from Clacton that its lifeboat, the *Albert Edward*, had reached the wreck the night before but could not get near enough to be of help. It had anchored off the sand till daylight, so near that the lifeboatmen could see and hear very early in the morning one of the masts crash overboard with survivors still clinging to it. Then all the lights they had seen on the wreck flickered and went out. The men of the *Albert Edward* guessed that was the end of the story. Unable to approach any closer to make absolutely sure they returned to Clacton having spent a full 24 hours facing the rigours of rain, wind and sea. Pulling most of the time, sailing where they could, they were exhausted.

That was not the end of the story. Down at Ramsgate they had seen the signals and hastily prepared to answer the call. The lifeboat, the *Bradford* was towed out against that stiff east wind by the steam paddle tug *Vulcan*. The discomfort and the danger in being towed through such stormy seas can hardly be imagined. By five o'clock that night they had reached the Kentish Knock lightship. Waiting until they got near enough and were more or less at the same height in the towering waves, they hailed her and got directions for the *Indian Chief*. They came as close as they dared to the edge of the sand, but by now it was too dark to discern the wreck. They burned their own recognition lights – hand-held green flares, but they got no response. They called up the tug, which backed to slacken the tow and bring them alongside and the coxswain said it would be best to lie-to through the night and see what they could see when dawn broke. It was too dangerous to anchor, for if the anchors dragged the *Vulcan* and the *Bradford* could be swept into the maelstrom of the shallows, so the *Vulcan* kept steam up and its paddles turning just enough to maintain its position against wind and current all through the night.

Unknown to them at that time there was still life on the *Indian Chief*. Before dark they had tried to get three of their own boats away. The first filled and sank immediately, the second had only two men in it when it broke away and was swamped. The men simply disappeared. The third boat was swamped even as it was lowered. That was the end of their escape bid. Whilst the *Bradford* was arriving in the gloom of gathering night, the *Indian Chief* was swept fore and aft by a mighty wave which left the deckhouses in splinters. The captain shouted to the crew to take to the rigging of the mizzen mast because he thought it was the sturdiest place of refuge. Seventeen of them lashed themselves in with rope they had cut from the rigging so that the mighty waves could not wash them off their precarious perches. The ship had by now broken its back on the sand so the mainmast, normally biggest and strongest, was no longer firmly secured and could not be trusted to resist the onslaught. Five men, not hearing the captain's advice, or not being able to make their way aft,

61

took to the platform halfway up the foremast, called the foretop. The mate following his captain to the mizzen then decided that the foremast was the safest place. Like a monkey he swung and climbed through rigging and up and down stays to get into the foretop with the other five.

The mainmast fell at three in the morning, and in its crashing down it caught and carried away all but the stump of the mizzen mast. Only the captain was left lashed to that stump. The other 15 men, lashed in the rigging so securely were swept away in a tangle of masts, spars and cordage to a terrible death. This incident was what the crew of the *Albert Edward* had seen from a distance, which made them think there was no hope of finding any survivors. When, in the dawn, the *Bradford* reached the *Indian Chief* they saw the captain swinging from the mizzen; the seas roaring over the wreck moved his legs to and fro. It looked as though he was struggling to free himself and make for the lifeboat. As they drew nearer the lifeboatmen could see from his hanging head and staring, sightless eyes that he was dead.

With infinite skill they negotiated the tangle of wreckage to get alongside and rescue the mate and those men in the rigging of the foremast. Altogether twelve men were rescued though one died almost immediately in the lifeboat. Then the tow was picked up from the *Vulcan* and a very cramped and uncomfortable journey for rescued and rescuers brought them to Ramsgate, to warm, dry clothing, a hot meal, and, at last, a healing sleep. Surely this story stands as a great tribute to the seamanship, the perseverance, the love of their fellow men in distress, and the sheer courage of those lifeboatmen.

Just in case you are wondering what happened to the crew of the *Nymphaea*, which, when the *Springwell* found her was only masts and funnel above water, let me put your mind at rest. It turned out that, despite the raging seas, the *Nymphaea*'s crew got their ship's boat safely away and all of them reached another steamer anchored securely off the sands not so far away. That steamer upped anchor as soon as it could and their story had a happy ending on the quay at Gravesend.

The Lesson of the *Enterkin*

Until 1890 the only help the pulling/sailing lifeboats could get was a tow off the beach and out to the area of a wreck by one of the new steam tugs. There were a couple at the busy port of Harwich. Seeing their ability to go out in all weathers, the Royal National Lifeboat Institution was encouraged to introduce a steam lifeboat, the first ever in this country, built at Blackwall on the Thames and named the *Duke of Northumberland*. Before it was transferred to New Brighton in 1892 it had made more than a dozen rescue bids in appalling weather, bringing safely ashore at least 33 survivors. It had also played its part in towing out the old lifeboat when its shallow draught was essential to a rescue on a sandbank.

Even with the advent of the age of steam there were still heartbreaking inadequacies in the lifesaving service. One was the lack of communication between look-outs ashore and the outer lightships, and between those lightships themselves. There was a cable laid to the lighthouse which then stood on the Gunfleet sands southeast of Walton-on-the-Naze, but it was thought that visual signalling was sufficient to pass messages on out to the Sunk lightvessel and the Galloper some 23 miles out. However, it was not in the sunshine, or in balmy breezes that ships got into difficulty – it was in driving rain and snow, or in fog when visual signals could not be seen 15 yards, let alone 15 miles.

So the scene was set for the tragedy of the *Enterkin*. History does not reveal its size, but we know that it had a crew of 31 and hailed from an English port. She was sailing far off the Essex coast, yet still close to one of the sandbanks which made a maze of the approach to the North Sea. It was the Galloper, 30 miles and more east of Clacton. On a dark December night in 1891 *Enterkin* picked up the Galloper light. The captain, having established his position, decided to wear ship, that is, to turn round by bringing the ship's bows away from the wind. He had not given himself enough room. Before the manoeuvre was completed the ship struck the sands. That was about half past five on 11th December. The ship fired rockets to show it was in distress. A smack making its way to Ramsgate responded. It could not be of much help, but it did take a couple of hands and an apprentice. The rest of the crew were hopeful that their signals, repeated to the coast by the Galloper lightvessel, would bring further, swift relief as the tide ebbed.

There was no such luck. The distress signals were seen. The Galloper's rockets alerted the Long Sand lightship and its repetition of the signal was seen closer in by the Sunk lightvessel some 15 miles east of Frinton. Their rockets were seen by the Cork lightship, stationed some eight miles off Landguard Point. That was how the Harwich look-out at last got the news and alerted the lifeboat. Out went the *Duke of Northumberland* – but just where were the wrecked mariners to be found? She headed for the Cork lightship.

Meanwhile the tide had ebbed; the *Enterkin*, left increasingly high and dry, fell on its side on the sand. As the tide rose the crew found perching points where they could on the uppermost side and yards of the stricken ship. There was no sign of rescue at hand. The tide rose inexorably, the wind reached gale force and piled up the

The RNLI's first steam lifeboat, *The Duke of Northumberland*, made many successful rescue bids in the most terrible conditions at the end of the 19th century. Sadly, it arrived too late to save those aboard the *Enterkin*, wrecked in December 1891.

waves on the cruel Galloper shallows. One man after another was plucked from his perch by a vicious rolling wave with the force of a battering ram.

At the Cork lightship the steam lifeboat had to risk an approach close enough to shout the question 'Where's the ship?' and to receive the answer that it was somewhere beyond the Sunk. Off set the lifeboat again for at least another hour's steaming against rough seas. At the Sunk it took time to make close enough contact to ask the question again – and again they were directed on, out to the Galloper lightvessel. Another 20 miles of rough water were traversed by the *Duke of Northumberland* and again she had to lay-to in hailing distance of the lightship to get the wreck's true bearing.

It was too late – all that effort was to no avail. The wreck was hardly showing above the waves – and there was no sign of human life amongst the flotsam. The *Duke of Northumberland*'s crew came back sad and feeling so frustrated; if the signals had been seen by the Shipwash light and sent on to Aldeburgh the lifeboat there could have been on the scene in just two and a half hours. The tragedy caused a reporter for the county newspaper to write:

'It was Henry Winstanley, of Littlebury, who led the progress in the provision of lighthouses, dying in his own Eddystone Lighthouse when it was swept away by a storm in 1703. It was Lionel Lukin of Dunmow who was the first to build a self-righting lifeboat in 1785. Another Essex man, George Palmer of Nazeing Park improved the design of the lifeboat – cannot a fourth Essex man devise some means of communication with our lightships?'

The answer was – Yes! Within ten years of this doleful disaster Marconi, not a native of the county but with his headquarters at Chelmsford, had sent wireless messages across the Atlantic and was soon making the wireless transmitting and receiving sets which meant that man need never again be alone upon the sea.

The Shipwrecked Pianos

She was a beautiful ship, the *Hawksdale*, a full-rigged vessel of 1,723 tons. She looked splendid in the sunshine with her clouds of white sail billowing out against the blue sky and a great curl of white foam creaming away under her prow against the blue sea. But what a responsibility a ship of this size was for its captain. With so much money invested in the building of the ship and in every cargo it carried there was great pressure on the captain and his crew to see the ship safely to its destination and the cargo unloaded into warehouses ashore.

The *Hawksdale*'s home port was Liverpool, but in January 1899 it was taking on a general cargo in Hamburg. It included furniture of all kinds and a special consignment of no less than 500 pianos. All this furniture was bound for the Australian market through the port of Melbourne. The North Sea had no great terrors for the experienced captain; in any case, he had a pilot on board to see him safely through the sandbanks off East Anglia and into the English Channel. It may be that the pilot had become blasé about a trip undertaken so many times that it was no more than a boring duty. Whatever the reason, the fact was that the *Hawksdale* was ghosting through the night of 25th–26th January when it grounded on the Long Sand. Later, survivors said they thought that the pilot, seeing the gleam of the lightvessel off the Kentish Knock, reckoned it was a light on the French coast.

With that light to port he steered a little to starboard to keep well offshore, but actually he had the *Hawksdale* running down the Knock Deep, heading directly for the Long Sand. There was no great panic. It was a big ship and the crew were not in immediate danger. Rockets of distress were fired high up in the night sky. At the same time an attempt was made to launch a boat in which two seamen and the pilot were to make for shore and lead rescuers to the wreck. Sad to say the boat capsized in the choppy sea where the tide rushed over the sands, the men were flung out, and they did not surface again within view of the *Hawksdale*.

That was a waste of three lives as it turned out, for their distress rockets had been seen on shore in places as far apart as Clacton and Margate.

From those two places lifeboats were launched on 26th January 1899. At Clacton it was the *Albert Edward*, the second boat to bear that name, now built to a brand new design which included a drop keel. The crew swore by it, said it sailed like a yacht and could go just about anywhere where there was a puddle of water. They sailed it out to the *Hawksdale*, picked up 18 of the crew without mishap and brought the total number of lives saved by this boat to 122 since its launch in 1885.

The Margate lifeboat was not long after the *Albert Edward* in reaching the wreck and taking off the remaining seven members of the crew. Now the ship was officially abandoned the 'salvagers' stepped in. One of them was Fred Salmon, who owned the *Emily*. He went to and fro for days, hoisting out cargo into his capacious smack. It included all kinds of furniture from lamps to what-nots, not forgetting those pianos which it seems, despite the movement of the waves and wind, were got on board the smack and taken in triumph to Brightlingsea. At that port the insurers arranged a special sale of the vast quantity of goods recovered. The smacksmen, who had made difficult and dangerous trips out to the wreck and had used up much time and energy in hoisting the heavier items out of the *Hawksdale* to bring them safely ashore as official salvagers, were awarded an agreed proportion of their value.

The end of the story can be read in the pages of the *Essex County Chronicle* for 3rd February 1899, where it is reported: 'On Friday afternoon the crew of the Clacton lifeboat, together with the rescued crew, were entertained to luncheon at the Grand Hotel, Clacton, by Mr H. Grant, as a mark of his appreciation of the gallant services rendered by the lifeboat men, and sympathy with the rescued. Music was discoursed by the lady orchestra attached to the hotel. Mr Harry Randall, a gentleman staying at the hotel, made both crews a present of £5 each.

'The same evening the shipwrecked men left for London. The captain spoke in high terms of the skilful manner in which the coxswain (Mr W. Scholfield) and the crew brought the lifeboat alongside the ship under such difficult and dangerous conditions.'

The salvage smacks which recovered so much of the cargo worked under a system of salvage which evolved early in the 19th century, reached its peak 50 years later and was rendered redundant by the end of the century when sail was giving way to steam and a much more exact control of a ship could be exercised through the improved equipment introduced on the bridge and in the engine-room. We have seen in the first chapter how, from the earliest days of sea trade, ships were at the mercy of severe storms. It was not long before brokers came forward to offer insurance on ships and their cargoes. A natural comcomitant was the payment in agreed proportion for any ships or cargoes recovered from groundings, collisions and other marine mishaps.

Full-rigged ships always conjure up a picture of white sails billowing against a blue sky sailing gracefully through the ocean. But the *Hawksdale*'s last voyage was very different. She met her fate on the treacherous sandbanks off the East Anglian coast on a winter's night in 1899.

The men most able to do the work of salvage were the fishermen along the coast of East Anglia. They had stout smacks built to withstand the battering of the North Sea in their quest for the cod which gained both men and boats the nickname of 'codbangers'. What is more they had the intimate knowledge of the sandbanks and shoals, their changes after every storm, and the variations of tide. Such men were tough – they would go out in a storm to a wreck, rescue the crew where possible, and strip the ship of everything of value, because it made more money in much less time than fishing.

For the most part the salvage was honest and official. There were regulations issued under an Act of Parliament in the 1820s which laid down that, amongst other places in the kingdom, Harwich, Brightlingsea and Wivenhoe were ports where salvaged cargo and wreckage was to be landed and registered. Naturally there were times when smacks took into their home ports equipment like anchors, cordage, fittings and the like which they could share amongst themselves or sell to fellow mariners. They might have found perishable fruit, meat or other food which would have gone bad before they could claim salvage – and there were hungry mouths at home.

The officials who had to see fair play in this matter of salvage were the local customs officers. They had to live in the communities which depended on the harvest of the sea – whatever that might be – and there were many days in the year when fishing was impossible, so they had a very difficult path to tread. No doubt there were times when they looked the other way as a smack or yawl landed the odd anchor, a few yards of cable, a ship's lantern or two. But it was apparent to all when the rockets went up and the smacks were hauled through the breakers that there was human salvage to be made before the idea of a little looting could be entertained. If they were accused of plunder the smacksmen could say that they were intending to take it all to the official receiver.

As trade increased through the middle years of the 19th century the salvagers were sailing out time and again to the rescue of the shipwrecked, and rewarding themselves with rich pickings. The situation is summed up by the late Hervey Benham in *The Salvagers* who wrote that in 1825:

'...smacksmen were warned off five wrecks on the Gunfleet and the Buxey, and another that had occurred on the Tongue in the same gales, but how many of these were specialist salvagers is impossible to determine. There is a suggestion in many of the accounts that the casuals behaved more rapaciously than the regulars. For example, when the brig *Lochiel* was wrecked on the Maplins in 1840 it was claimed she was looted by smacksmen, "except Captain Eagle of the *George and Eliza* of Wivenhoe and Captain Andrews of the *Fair Traveller* of Colchester."'

By 1830 a number of fishermen along the whole coast had given up fishing to become full-time salvagers. When a regular treasure trove of a ship went aground on the sands miles offshore a veritable fleet of smacks would home in on it. Forty five of them surrounded the *Ariel*, aground on the Gunfleet in 1846. In 1861, as we have seen in a previous chapter, some 30 salvagers raced out to the *Regina.*

As time went on the professional salvager adapted his boat, even adding diving equipment. The Suffolk and Norfolk salvagers swore by their yawls, open boats which were launched off the beach. They formed 'companies' of men working as teams in keen rivalry and very closely controlled. Some of them went so far as to have printed rules of membership. The Caister Company of Beachmen's rules have been set out in full in Robert Malster's *Saved From the Sea* (1974). The first rule declares: 'Every man who shall touch any Coble, Gig, Yawl, or outrigger of the same, or any boat, belonging to or in the use of the Company, as she is going off to any vessel, shall be considered as belonging to that boat, and shall be entitled to an equal share of the earnings and emoluments of the boat, to which he shall thus be considered to belong.' These rules also looked after the interests of widows and children of company men who lost their lives on the job.

Such companies had their craft specially built for the purpose. Some were up to 70 feet long, equally sharp at bow and stern and well on the slim side. They cut the water like a knife. They had up to nine thwarts for the oarsmen when the wind was contrary, and sails of a size which made them the biggest open sailing boats of their day. The attitude of the salvagers of East Anglia can be summed up by a quotation from Robert Malster's book:

'Small wonder that the beachmen gained a reputation among other seamen as "longshore sharks", for they were always watching from their lookouts perched above the marram hills or on the cliff·for vessels in trouble. Lest it be thought that the beachmen were mere parasites, however, one should remember the words of J. Haylett, the famous Caister beachman and lifeboatman, during a salvage case many years ago. When asked if it was not true that other people's misfortunes were the beachmen's opportunities, he replied, "No, their mistakes." '

Shipwrecked Off Canvey

It is nearly 90 years since Canvey Island saw its celebrated shipwreck. Actually nobody saw it because it happened in one of the pea-souper fogs which in those days drifted down on the wind from the smoke-laden skies of London. On a mighty cold morning in January 1902, the steamship *Ben Mohr*, 3,000 tons, was groping its way down the estuary, bound for far-off India with a cargo of Portland cement in barrels loaded the day before at London docks.

Captain Wallace had the added responsibility of a couple of passengers on the long trip, but he was an experi-

This artist's impression of the wreck of the *Ben Mohr* appeared in one of the first published guides to Canvey Island. Barges are engaged in salvaging the sunken cargo.

75

enced sailor, used to the run and familiar with the winding waterway. He stayed in the wheelhouse, supporting the crew on watch, not looking for landmarks but listening for those noises which led fog-blinded shipping on down the Thames. Ships' sirens sounded their approach, and they kept a healthy distance in response to *Ben Mohr*'s moaning response. From its position on the Chapman sands, stretching eastward from Canvey Point, the Chapman lighthouse added its wailing warning to the chorus. The captain was not too worried; he had worked the *Ben Mohr* down the Thames in conditions like this time and again. Everybody on board was looking forward to sailing south to the sun.

It was a terrible shock when the steamship *Banffshire* suddenly loomed up over them out of the fog. A collision was inevitable, the *Ben Mohr*'s crew literally saw it coming. With the massive bulk of the *Banffshire* grinding into the plates of the *Ben Mohr* there was, for a moment, consternation. Some members of the crew would have panicked but for Captain Wallace's quick reactions. He calmly issued orders, settling the crew down to managing the situation just as he commanded them. He knew his ship had been badly holed and would quickly sink in the deep fairway if he did not act quickly. He had the wheel put over to hard a-port and rang the telegraph to the engine room 'Full speed ahead'. While the *Banffshire* resumed its proper course and was soon lost again in the fog, the *Ben Mohr* veered out of the main channel and drove hard up on the muddy shore off Hole Haven and in sight of the famous old Lobster Smack Inn, featured in Dickens' stories.

The engines were stopped, the crew and passengers ordered on deck, and the ship was abandoned in orderly fashion. The news of the collision had been received by the coastguard station close by on Canvey and the men and

Holidaymakers to Canvey Island had their photograph taken on the concrete 'barrels' recovered from the *Ben Mohr's* cargo of cement.

77

their wives were soon down on the foreshore to offer assistance to the crew and those poor, confused passengers.

Thus the human cargo was saved, though horribly shocked. What about that cargo of cement? I am sorry to say that, such is the character of cement, there was nothing that could be done about it. It had started to solidify in the barrels as soon as it came into contact with the water, down in the hold. But in its solidified state it still had some value. Since a new pier was then in course of construction at the eastern end of the island, and good hardcore was at a premium, a speculator bought up all *Ben Mohr*'s solid barrels of Thames-set concrete and had them hoisted out of the ship and into a barge which dumped them on the beach by the projected pier. He made a handsome profit but the builders of the pier did not; they went broke and the pier was never finished.

Those strangely-shaped lumps of concrete stayed there, washed by the tide, greened by seaweed, encrusted with molluscs, until they looked like some weird southern outcrop of the Giants Causeway. As late as 1970 it was reported that some of these 'stones' still had clinging to them the staves of the original barrels. Apparently there are still one or two of them to be seen today, but you have to look in the right place. Other people say that they were absorbed in the sea wall when it was considerably raised in height in recent years to allow for any contingencies arising from the closure of the London Barrage, in the event of London being threatened by floods.

The *Ben Mohr* suffered the indignity of looting by souvenir hunters as it lay just offshore, but it did not rust away here at Canvey. It was recovered a few months later, towed to a Tyneside shipyard and repaired. Good as new, it carried on trading to India and the Far East, where it was sold to a Japanese shipping company in 1911. Strange to relate, the old *Ben Mohr* met its fate 25 years after the Canvey collision, to the very month. In January 1927 it was driven aground off Japan and that was its last resting place.

The Harwich Force

There are forces other than natural disasters which can wreck a ship. We are not talking about human error, in navigation or in seamanship, but about purposeful ship-wreck, in war, by an enemy. The futility and sadness of such shipwreck is fully illustrated in just one example.

A state of war had been declared between Germany and Great Britain on 4th August 1914. At a very early hour the next day the people of Harwich, including many a sailor's wife and mother, crowded on the quay and all along the sea front to see the Harwich Force go steaming out of the harbour at high speed. There was great, cheering enthu-siasm shown by these crowds of onlookers as our Royal Navy went out to find and fight the enemy.

The Harwich Force was then made up of the cruisers *Arethusa, Fearless, Undaunted* and *Aurora* which, together with 40 destroyers were formed into two flotillas. There were always a number of these ships with steam up, ready to leave at a moment's notice. Even when the situation was not urgent the longest notice to sail given to the Force throughout the war was just three hours. E. F. Knight has written, 'Harwich, possibly, was nearer to the war and its tragedies than any other port in England.'

So, at 6 a.m. the Force left harbour and fanned out across the ocean into its hunting packs. One section of destroyers led by the light cruiser *Amphion* was near the Galloper lightship when the cruiser's Captain Fox made the signal, 'Good Hunting!' The *Amphion*, displacement

3,440 tons, mounted ten four-inch guns. Launched in 1911, it had a top speed of 25½ knots.

On this brilliant August day of shining sun and shimmering sea it fell to this flotilla to fire the first shots at sea in the Great War. At 10.30 the *Konigin Luise*, a German mail steamer converted to a minelayer, was sighted afar off. The destroyers *Lance* and *Landrail* were sent off in pursuit and to block her escape. The destroyers *Lark* and *Linnet* then arrived on the scene and a fierce action commenced.

By noon the flotilla had come up in strength but the minelayer, already badly damaged by gunfire was limping away, her speed drastically reduced.

At 2.15 p.m. she was in such a perilous condition that the crew abandoned ship by jumping overboard. They did not even wait until the engines were stopped, and so the *Konigin Luise* went slowly on ahead until she filled so full that the engine room was flooded and the fires under her boilers were extinguished. Then she turned on her side and slowly sank. Of her crew of 100, only 23 were picked up by boats from the destroyers and 20 by those from the *Amphion*, and some of them were badly wounded. But that was not the end of the story.

The minelayer had evidently done its work before it was sighted for, at 6.35 a.m. on the following morning, the *Amphion* struck one of its mines. The impact appeared to be directly under the forebridge. Every sailor on the forward messdecks was killed along with 18 of the Germans they had rescued. Captain Fox and the four other officers on the bridge were badly burnt and very shocked. The *Amphion* began to settle in the water, down by the head. Already the fires raging in the lower decks had turned the bows dull red and black with the intense heat. Her steering was gone; she circled slowly for a few minutes until order could be restored and 'Stop engines' could be implemented. The crew were ordered to assemble on the quarterdeck. There was no panic. With the discipline of the parade ground the boats were lowered and boats from the accompanying destroyers were soon alongside. All the survivors of that dreadful blast were saved.

From the decks of the destroyers they watched the dying moments of their ship. The fires raging under the foredecks reached the magazines and a terrific explosion occurred. It blew away most of the bows and the forepart of the *Amphion*. The falling wreckage spread so far that it caused further casualties on the destroyers. One shell, blown straight out of the *Amphion*'s magazine, fell on the *Lark* and killed three men who had only just been rescued. Two were of the *Amphion*'s crew. The third was a German. He had survived two terrible shipwrecks in less than 24 hours only to be killed by this coincidence of falling debris.

The story ends with a football. Men pulling one of the boats from a destroyer looking for possible survivors in a sea of wreckage, saw a football bobbing about amongst it, quite undamaged, having been blown clean out of the *Amphion*. It affected them so deeply that they stopped, fished it out and used it with pride whenever the destroyers were in port long enough to fix up a football match.

So this first naval action of the First World War left two more wrecks to litter the seabed off the East Anglian coast. Winston Churchill put it all in perspective in his *World Crisis*, summing up the start of the war at sea: 'So we waited; and nothing happened. No great event immediately occurred. No battle was fought. The Grand Fleet remained at sea: the German Fleet did not quit the shelter of its harbours. There were no cruiser actions. A German minelayer sowing a minefield off Harwich was chased and sunk by a flotilla of destroyers led by *Amphion*; and the *Amphion* returning, was blown up on the German minefield. Otherwise silence unbroken by cannon brooded over the broad and narrow waters.'

The Ship That Split In Two

The Dutch-registered oil tanker *Georgia*, 5,111 tons, had taken on a full consignment of oil at Abadan in the Persian Gulf and had almost completed its journey to Grangemouth in Scotland when it ran into a storm force gale off the Norfolk coast around midnight on 21st November 1927. That was the moment when the steering gear chose to break down irreparably. The tanker drifted helplessly before the storm blowing out of the south and hit the Happisburgh (pronounced Hazeborough) Sands seven miles north-northwest of the Newarp lightship. That same wind was piling up waves like battering rams across the shallow water over the sands. Even though the tanker was made of steel it was smashed into two separate pieces by this onslaught. The bow section was washed by its own weight deeper and deeper into the sands. The stern section, still in deeper water, was wrenched from it and swept away, with the wind and tide pushing it towards Cromer.

The *Georgia* had a wireless operator, but the sequence of events was so swift that the grounding came and the aerials were broken and blown away before he could so much as get a finger on the Morse Code transmitter button. Not one crew member was lost as the two halves of the tanker parted. So there, on the sandbank, Captain Harry Kissing and 14 members of the crew huddled together in the shelter of the forecastle, watching the waves break clear across the deck, foaming white in the darkness of the night. They could only hope that some other vessel had seen their plight and would report their position.

Actually it was the stern section, with the remaining 16 members of the crew on board which was first sighted, but that was not until it had drifted northwestwards all through the night. Daylight at last brought them glorious relief. Around eight o'clock they were sighted by a look-out on the SS *Trent*. She was able to lower a boat and, with fine seamanship, take off all 16 men without mishap. When the captain of the *Trent* heard the account of the grounding of the forward end of the *Georgia* he set off for the Happisburgh Sands at once, at the same time transmitting requests for help from other vessels in the vicinity and from the Coastguard.

The lifeboat station at Great Yarmouth heard the call and went into action. They launched the lifeboat *John and Mary Meiklam* which after a very rough two-hour journey made a rendezvous with the *Trent*. Nearby the bow section of the *Georgia* was being pounded by a sea so violent that even the coxswain of the lifeboat did not dare to risk the lives of his men in a rescue attempt. Night came on, the storm did not abate. All the lifeboat could do was to moor in the lee of the *Trent* and wait. In the dawn of the following day the lifeboatmen made any number of attempts at getting a line across the wreck. At last they succeeded and a two-inch hawser was reeved to it. Before the shipwrecked men could scramble down it a mighty wave pounded down, swamped the wreck and snapped the rope as if it were cotton thread. By this time the lifeboatmen were exhausted by the buffeting they had taken through more than 24 hours. They headed back to Yarmouth for a complete change of clothes and a well-earned meal.

Quite separately, fishermen off Cromer spotted the after

The motor-driven lifeboat *John and Mary Meiklam*. It went to the rescue of the oil tanker *Georgia* which split in two during a storm in 1927.

section of the *Georgia*, still afloat and drifting further and further away from the coast. They were not to know that there was no longer anyone on board. They called out the lifeboat from Cromer, the *H. F. Bailey*, at around two in the morning. Those brave and skilled lifeboatmen found that wreck in the wild wastes of the North Sea, boarded it, checked there was nobody left on board and, judging it to be a hazard to shipping, stood by it through the rest of the night. After 16 hours at sea they handed over the watch on the wreck to Cromer's other lifeboat, the *Louisa Heartwell*.

But the crew of the *H. F. Bailey* did not find the rest and refreshment they so richly deserved; it was necessary to go out at once and check on a rowing boat drifting down the coast. They reached it, found it unmanned, simply set adrift, and when they came in from that search they were asked to go straight out to the Happisburgh Sands to relieve the *John and Mary Meiklam* which, all this time, had been standing by the *Georgia*'s bow section stuck on the sands. The weather was still extremely bad and its coxswain had judged any attempt at rescue foolhardy.

The *H. F. Bailey* was commanded by the great Henry Blogg, famous among seamen the world over for his daring and his bravery in countless rescues at sea. He did not want to expose his crew to another night of danger and wretchedness out in the storm. The light was going early on that grim and gloomy November day. Henry Blogg took the lifeboat straight through the awe-inspiring surf which raged round the wreck. With superb seamanship by him and his crew the lifeboat was brought right alongside the wreck for a brief moment; long enough to get lines thrown up to the deck which were fastened by the *Georgia*'s crew, who then lowered themselves and dropped safely into the lifeboat.

It was but the matter of a few seconds to check all were aboard and cut the lines, but in that brief space of time a huge wave came sweeping in and lifted the lifeboat up and up on to the edge of the *Georgia*'s deck. In that deathly pause when the lifeboat's fate hung in the balance the engineman proved himself. He whipped the engines into reverse as the next huge wave came tearing in. The propellers dug in, the boat pulled away. It was badly damaged, holed and waterlogged, but the engines just kept going. When at last the *H. F. Bailey* crawled into Gorleston its crew had been on duty continuously for 28 hours. That is what I call devotion to duty. All the lifeboat men involved in this heroic rescue received awards for gallantry from the Royal National Lifeboat Institution.

The Stranded Bomb

The Second World War in Europe was drawing to a close. On 22nd January 1944 the Allied forces had landed at Anzio. On 6th June, D-Day, more than 4,000 ships took part in the invasion of Europe. The ammunition expended in horrific engagements like the capture of Caen required supplies on a vast scale. One ship that brought a huge cargo of bombs, detonators and other explosives from the United States of America was the *Richard Montgomery*, named after an 18th century American patriot.

It had eluded the U-Boats and survived the vagaries of the Atlantic and had reached the outer waters of the Thames estuary. It was under orders to meet up with the convoy then assembling off Southend to be shepherded to the recently liberated port of Cherbourg, where its cargo would make a valuable contribution to the Allied advance. But the *Richard Montgomery* fell at the very last hurdle. On 20th August 1944, and at the top of a spring tide, she went aground on the Sheerness Middle Sand, more or less in the middle of the Thames estuary, a mile and a half off Sheerness and only 235 yards north of the important sea lane into the Thames, called the Medway Approach Channel.

This was a really difficult problem for the authorities. The crew were safely evacuated in good weather and the salvage experts were called in. They reported that if she was to be refloated it would only be by removing some of

The wreck of the *Richard Montgomery* as it appears today off Sheerness. She posed severe problems to the authorities when she went down in the Second World War with a cargo of volatile explosives and bombs. (Reproduced by kind permission of Geoff Baker)

her cargo, to make her float higher in the water, and then waiting for the next spring, or extra high, tide. Within three days of going aground the *Richard Montgomery* was surrounded by ships and barges and men were busy as bees on her deck. The situation was desperate because some of the ship's plates had already buckled under the strain of settlement in the sand. Three thousand tons of the volatile cargo of heavy and dangerous bombs and other explosives had been carefully hoisted out and sent ashore when the worst possible thing happened; the ship settled further in the sands. The strain broke her back forward of the bridge and the holds were instantly flooded. Some 3,700 tons of explosive material had to be abandoned in what was now a total wreck.

During the period of clearing up wrecks and other obstructions round the coast in the wake of the Second World War, the *Richard Montgomery* was inspected by explosives experts who reported in 1952 that such a dangerous wreck was best left alone. There was however some strong local feeling that the wreck was a great threat to people around Sheerness on the Kent coast, in that nearly 4,000 tons of bombs remained in the holds. If they were by some freak chance exploded simultaneously there would be an unparalleled explosion. An article in the journal of the Port of London Authority summed up the situation in 1973: 'The wreck has provided the subject of a lengthy argument waged for many years between those who feel that active measures should be taken to ensure that the *Richard Montgomery* constitutes no threat to safety, and those who feel that the wreck should be left undisturbed.'

But the matter had not been allowed to rest there. The situation was reviewed again in 1964 by a working party from all the authorities involved. They asked for a full diving survey – and when the Royal Navy divers reported back they confirmed the working party's opinion – leave well alone! The watchful eye of the British government did not close however, even though the *Richard Montgomery* was, technically, still owned by the United States of America. In 1971 a study was commissioned to judge whether the wreck should be protected from the possibility of other ships, out of control, drifting into it and causing a cataclysmic explosion. The arguments against such extra protection included the difficulty of keeping such a barrier in place and the interference it would impose in the tidal flow. What is more, if the barrier broke up in storm or collision it could be driven out into the Medway Approach Channel, to the great hazard of shipping.

Another survey in 1965 showed the ship had silted up considerably and its fore part had heeled over another four degrees. The divers were forbidden to enter the wreck, in the interest of their own safety as well as because there was a possibility that they could accidentally cause the cargo to explode.

The risk of spontaneous explosion, however, had become remote. On 13th August 1981, 37 years almost to the day after it went aground, the *Richard Montgomery* was inspected once again by diving teams from the Royal Navy and Ministry of Defence. This time they went into the holds and actually touched one of the bombs. They used ultrasonic and underwater television equipment in the most rigorous examination of all the five surveys. The naval lieutenant in charge is quoted as saying, 'We do not regard the ammunition as in a dangerous condition. It is certainly no more dangerous than the mines and old bombs we have to deal with every day.'

So, the wreck still lies there undisturbed. Time has passed to the extent that the records of the *Richard Montgomery* have been handed from the Port of London Authority to the Museum of London, where the librarian writes, 'The wreck is very well marked by large yellow buoys and has been so long in situ that it is a landmark.' It should be added that the buoys are illuminated at night, a foghorn operates automatically and the Thames river patrol keeps a constant eye on the situation. As *The Times* newspaper noted: 'The cost of keeping ships away from the wreck and the numerous surveys has so far run into millions of pounds. The Government has taken direct responsibility for the ship, although it is still in dispute with the United States about who should be responsible.' And so the saga of the *Richard Montgomery* goes on.

And There Flowed
An Orange Tide

Yarmouth and oranges have a double connection as far as shipwrecks are concerned. Twice the good folk of Yarmouth have been able to gather from the sea a strange harvest of thousands and thousands of oranges.

The first time was before the First World War when a ship, whose name has long been forgotten, piled up on the sands off Yarmouth. In those days dwellers in the Norfolk countryside seldom saw an orange. Their money was spent on the more important necessities of life; oranges appeared in Christmas stockings as a special treat.

So the news of oranges washing ashore spread like wildfire and hundreds of people were soon scrambling in and out of the waves, filling all kinds of containers from handcarts and barrows to coats and jerseys with their sleeves and necks tied up with string to form makeshift sacks. Though the oranges had floated in from a sandbank some miles out their skins had rendered them impervious to any damage from salt water.

It happened again some 50 years later when, in December 1948, the steamer *Bosphorous* hit the Haisbro Sands whilst carrying a cargo of oranges destined for Sunderland. This time the oranges were dumped overboard on purpose, in order that the ship could be lightened sufficiently to be towed off at the next high tide. Those oranges drifted ashore by the thousand; one local inhabitant remembered how it seemed like a gift from God – apparently the Ministry of Food had just informed the Yarmouth area that there would be no quota of oranges that Christmas – and here they were making their own way ashore.

When this lady went down to the beach at six o'clock in the morning for her usual constitutional she saw 'a wide band of oranges stretching north and south as far as the eye could see.' Since she ran a greengrocery business this was an opportunity not to be missed. She thought of all the children of her regular customers – how they would just love to have a Christmas orange. But how to collect them? December it was, cold and windy, but she took off her coat, tied the sleeve-ends and filled them with oranges. Then, buttoning it up, she filled the whole body of the coat. She struggled with this load across the beach and into the road. By this time her husband was worried about her prolonged absence. Heading down the road to the beach, he saw his wife coming towards him, lugging what he thought was a dead body!

Since she had already collected enough oranges for her customers' children, she did the decent thing and went round her neighbourhood knocking on doors where she knew there were families with young children. In no time at all there was a procession of prams, pushchairs, handcarts and wheelbarrows heading for the beach to reap that most unlikely harvest, still washing in like an orange tide. How true the old proverb is, 'It's an ill wind that blows nobody any good' – and that was in spite of the Customs officers' warning that all oranges must be handed in – as salvage!

Swallowed by the Scroby Sand

The Times of 5th December 1950 put it very simply.
'Trawler stranded off Great Yarmouth. Gorleston lifeboat
and the Great Yarmouth tug *Richard Lee Barber* went
through snow showers in the North Sea last night to the
help of the Ostend trawler *Yarmouth* which had run
aground on Scroby Sand between three and four miles
from the shore opposite Great Yarmouth.' It did not
comment on the strange coincidence that a Belgian trawler, for some unaccountable reason named *Yarmouth*,
should end up high and dry in full view of the celebrated
fishing port of the same name.

Legend has it that the Scroby Sand was once an island in
the sea. A vicious storm blew up, fierce beyond all remem-
brance, and the island was washed away. The everchang-
ing nature of the sandbanks off East Anglia, shifting at the
whim of tide and current, and the action of wind and wave
has led to the re-accumulation of the Scroby Sand to the
extent that there is dry land even at high tide, and terns are
known to have nested there.

They must have been surprised when the *Yarmouth*
intruded upon their sanctuary. She did not drive in deep
and firm but banged and bumped upon the sands,
pounded by rolling waves until the tide receded. The call
for help brought the *Louise Stephens* out of the Gorleston

lifeboathouse. To her crew this was just another rescue, though never could the ever-present risk of injury or even death allow any rescue to be called routine. The sea was so rough on the sands that the first attempt to reach the wreck had to be abandoned. But a second and successful attempt was made in company with the tug *Richard Lee Barber*; the lifeboat training its searchlight on the wreck to enable the tug to manoeuvre alongside. The intention was to haul the *Yarmouth* off the sands at five in the morning, when the tide was at its highest.

As soon as they could approach over the sands the lifeboatmen took the crew aboard and landed them safely at Gorleston. The lifeboat had to cope with a snow squall which reduced visibility almost to nil. The sea was actually breaking over the trawler and the crew had to be snatched off it one by one as they literally jumped for their lives. For ten hours through the night the *Louise Stephens* and the *Richard Lee Barber* laboured at the rescue. This, carried out in total darkness, in bitter cold and heavy seas was simply described as 'a tricky job' by Coxswain Bert Beavers. The *Yarmouth Mercury* reported the difficult manoeuvre of getting alongside and taking off the crew as 'a hazardous job accomplished skilfully.'

The crew, then, were safe, but nothing could be done for the trawler. The effort to tow it off the sandbank was futile. The trawler's master, Arthur Verbeist, of Ostend was appreciative of all the efforts made. He explained that it was on the last leg of a round trip of 2,000 miles from Ostend to Iceland and back. It had been a good trip, they had 6,000 stones of white fish on board. It may have been the sheer weight of that cargo which led the *Yarmouth* to bed itself so firmly in the sand.

Ten days later the local paper had sadly to report, 'Belgian Trawler Still on Scroby.' Every day the lifeboat and tugs *Richard Lee Barber* and *George Jewson* had

The trawler *Yarmouth* ran aground on the Scroby Sand in a snow storm in 1950. Despite many efforts to refloat her, the shifting sands remain her grave to this day.

made attempts to move the *Yarmouth*. Most of her cargo of fish was taken off along with water and fuel in the hope that the reduced weight would give the tugs a chance to pull her free, but continuing bad weather interfered with the operation. One day, when the tide was low, the lifeboat got near enough to allow the trawler master, his mate and his chief engineer, together with two lifeboatmen, to lower a small boat and land on the sand. To get on to the trawler they had to wade waist-deep in the water, but they made it and got a winch going to secure a line. Then the weather closed in again! What is more, a lifeboatman was injured so it was back to base in a hurry, with the trawler's crew returning to their haven at the Shipwrecked Sailors' Home.

Refloating of the trawler now seemed more problematic than possible. When the storm blew itself out there was the *Yarmouth* still standing upright on the sand and showing her plimsoll line – looking virtually undamaged to the untutored eye. The salvage man knew otherwise, but he counted it still as a valuable prize if only he could get it into the deep channel and tow it to port. Through the winter and the spring there were many more attempts. Even the big Hull tug *Krooman* had no effect. The silent, sucking sand was the master.

The Scroby Sand keeps on the move, shape and size ever changing. The great storm of 1953, the extra high tide and the mighty wind caused the sands to shift dramatically. They engulfed the *Yarmouth*. It was reported in 1986 that all that could be seen of the *Yarmouth* then was the top of her cabin and part of her mast. Today the coxswain of the Gorleston lifeboat, Richard Hawkins, reports that those last signs of the wreck of the *Yarmouth* have disappeared.

Fire Afloat!

It was not a storm at sea, a collision or the shallows of a sandbank which wrecked the *Gudveig* on 3rd March 1961. It was that doubly-dreaded disaster, fire.

This 4,124 ton Norwegian cargo ship had reached the last few miles of its journey from Casablanca to Immingham in Lincolnshire with a cargo of phosphates and timber. It was around four o'clock in the morning when Norwegian Magne Skjerviek, in the engine room, and Englishman John Davis of Birmingham, on deck watch, almost simultaneously saw smoke and gave the alarm. Captain Borguald Solum summed up the situation and saw that help was needed immediately. Radio Officer Alnas sent out the call 'Fire in engine room', stating that the *Gudveig*'s position was then close to the North-East Cross Sand Buoy.

By the time the Caister and Great Yarmouth lifeboats were launched the crew of the *Gudveig* were vainly trying to contain a fire which spread so rapidly that flames were licking up over the top of the funnel. Meanwhile the London steamship *Tennyson* had heard the call and altered course to be of assistance. It stood by while 28 members of the *Gudveig*'s crew were brought across in the ship's boats. Among them was the only seawoman aboard, stewardess Asland Alnas, wife of the radio officer. He had to stay on board the stricken vessel, but more help was on its way. The Gorleston lifeboat came struggling through

Pressmen came to see the results of the heroic work by the firemen, lifeboatmen and crew when the *Gudveig* caught fire, carrying a cargo of phosphates
and timber in 1961 off the Norfolk coast.

the fog of this early March day when it was still only
barely light. Coxswain George Mobbs took the rescued
crew off the *Tennyson* and soon had them safely ashore at
Yarmouth.

By 8.30 a.m. the Lowestoft lifeboat had come alongside
the *Gudveig* with a contingent of firemen from the local
fire station. This was an historic occasion, for it was the
first time that firemen from a land-based station had been
taken out to sea to extinguish a fire on a ship. But it was
not plain sailing. Just when they thought they had everything under control the fire suddenly spread to the 200
tons of wood in the forward hold. This is where the
Gorleston lifeboat was able to help again. Having landed

the crew members it took on board twelve firemen from the Yarmouth Fire Brigade, under Station Officer Howes, and some extra pumps and so the Lowestoft firemen could be relieved.

The fire was dowsed at last, the ship was taken in tow to port and the Caister lifeboat took off all the rest of the crew who could be spared. That meant the radio officer came ashore at Caister while his wife was waiting for him at Yarmouth! After what they had been through that must have seemed only a minor inconvenience.

Captured on Camera

Even today photographs of shipwrecks as they actually happen are few and far between. Who wants to bother with a camera when there is a life on the line? But in the case of one ship from which all the crew had been saved, there was taken a sequence of photographs of the death of a ship which is far more expressive than the most inspired description in imaginative prose. The ship in question was the *Sea Rhine*, a 200 ton coaster with a cargo of steel coils, each weighing ten tons, bound from the Rhine to Boston, Lincolnshire. Its master was Mr Anthony Francis, a 30 year old Cornishman who was no stranger to the vagaries of the sea, for he had been shipwrecked before.

It was exactly 28 minutes past four on the stormy morning of 11th February 1976 that the Coastguard at Gorleston received the *Sea Rhine*'s call for help and re-layed it on the recently introduced Channel 16 'Mayday' waveband to the Gorleston lifeboat. This was the first time the new system had been put into practice for a real emergency. Brian Coleman, writing in *Coastguard*, explains the situation:

'We followed the procedure set out, things went smoothly, and we felt fully in control of the situation. The "Mayday" was answered correctly, relay broadcasts were issued as required, and the lifeboat duly went on its way. Response and co-operation from ships at sea, and from Humber Radio, were first class – everyone worked as a

Going, going, gone! Lifeboat coxswain Richard Hawkins photographed the final hours of the *Sea Rhine* after all the crew had been rescued.

team. We all felt that our more direct communication with the casualty and the other assisting vessels was a great advantage over the old indirect system of communications via Humber Radio.'

Richard Hawkins took the Gorleston lifeboat *Khami* out to his first rescue as its coxswain, though he had, of course, years of experience in the service at other stations. By the greatest of good luck he happened to take his camera with him. Some 18 miles east of Lowestoft the *Khami* came up with the *Sea Rhine*, and several tugs which were standing by their comrade in distress. One tug, the Liverpool-based *Crosbie*, had already cleverly man-oeuvred alongside the listing coaster and offered to take off the three-man crew. The master and the crewman took the chance and leapt aboard. The mate, Mr Sewell, de-cided to stay on board and make a last, despairing effort to save the *Sea Rhine* by bringing it to face dead into the wind and aiming for calmer, more shallow waters in the lee of the land. The gale worsened, however, and the heavy seas pounding the ship made the cargo shift a little more and so exaggerated the list.

At this time, we must remember, it was still dark enough for a Hercules aircraft from the American Air Force base at Woodbridge to be called to the scene and drop flares, while an RAF helicopter hovered over the vessel to snatch the mate if the worst came to the worst.

It was not required because the lifeboat had taken up a position about 20 ft from the *Sea Rhine*'s port quarter ready to close in and grab the mate the moment he decided to abandon ship. On the *Khami* they could hear the clanging of cargo and other loose equipment as the tired ship, almost overwhelmed, lifted sluggishly to each wave and fell, a deadweight, into the trough. The coaster listed further, to nearly 25°, and the mate saw that his ploy was unsuccessful. He had been all alone on the coaster for over an hour. Now it was time to give up. He signalled his surrender; Richard Hawkins brought the *Khami* right up to the port side of the *Sea Rhine* just forward of the stern. Mr Sewell jumped and the strong arms of a lifeboatman grabbed him and eased his landing. It transpired that he had been mate for only ten days, acting as a temporary relief. This modest man's comments on his efforts and experiences was; 'The emergency services moved very quickly and it was all very smooth.'

The *Sea Rhine* stayed afloat for another hour and a half, until at last it slid under the waves. As its mast showed just its tip, the hatches burst and a fountain of water forced up by the air in the hold signified the end of the emergency. While the lifeboat waited, ready to warn off shipping in the offing, Richard Hawkins pointed his camera and took an amazing sequence of pictures of the last moments of a sinking ship. This incident reflects clearly the wonderfully efficient, well-organised system of sea rescue which has so reduced the casualties in shipwrecks which sailing men a century ago had to take for granted.

The Great Oil Slick

On Saturday 6th May 1978 a Greek registered super-tanker, *Eleni V* was making its staid but powerful way from Rotterdam to Grangemouth. It had reached a point some four miles off Lowestoft when out of the mist there loomed another giant of the modern seaways, the *Roseline*, a French bulk ore carrier. For reasons inexplicable the *Roseline* did not see, until much too late, the long low outline of the *Eleni V*; it ploughed into it, through it, and left the tanker split into two pieces.

Thankfully, there were no human casualties. Thirty nine of the *Eleni V*'s crew abandoned ship in orderly fashion in two lifeboats and four were picked up by the *Roseline*, which transferred them to a lifeboat and then, having checked damage to herself, continued on her way. But there was a serious casualty in this collision. It was the whole environment, sea and land over a wide area around the wreck, for the tanker was still carrying 3,000 tons of oil, contained in the bow section which, having turned turtle, was yet still afloat, while the afterpart of the *Eleni V* drifted on to a sandbank three miles off Corton and sank.

So the problem focussed on that leaking bow section where three compartments, each holding a thousand tons of oil, were being so buffeted by huge waves heaped up in the shallows by rising winds at the change of the tide that they were leaking more and more oil. Within 48 hours the slick of escaping oil covered some 15,000 square metres, or, roughly, six square miles. The difficult job of coordinating efforts to contain the sinister, ever-spreading and suffocating oil-slick fell to the Coastguard centre at Gorleston. They acted quickly and commandeered five tugs, a trawler and a rig supply vessel to spray detergent on the oil. It was reckoned that the slick already represented a leak of a thousand tons of oil, but the spraying did break it up into smaller, more manageable slicks. They were now only a mile and a half off the coast. Norfolk and Suffolk County Councils and Yarmouth Borough Council got together to prepare a crisis plan of action if the oil did hit the beaches.

The hampering obstacle to an immediate clean-up was that the bow section, still afloat, rising out of the water like an enormous whale, was in the main shipping lane and could thus cause further collisions and catastrophe, especially through the night. Out at sea in cold and stormy waters and under most unpleasant conditions with oil all around them, divers were working to weld on to the bow another anchorage point for a second tow line so that she could be towed further inshore. When they received plans of the *Eleni V*, sent urgently from Greece, they found they had been using their welding torches directly on the side of a tank full of oil. The risk of an explosion was so great they had to start all over again in another area. It was a vital part of the strategy in dealing with the wreck because the strain of a single tow line at one point on the bows might pull the plating further apart, start another great flow of oil and so dramatically increase the pollution.

As it was, with more than 20 ships spraying away by 10th May, the oil still came ashore, fouling beaches and sea defences all the way from Yarmouth as far south as Aldeburgh and, eventually, well beyond that. A boom put across Great Yarmouth harbour by the Anglian Water

Authority broke under the strain and small patches of oil penetrated Breydon Water – the entrance to the Norfolk Broads. Further to the south the sticky oil threatened to block one of the cooling water pipelines at the Sizewell power station. Luckily the wind changed and the slick was moved on and away. Oil-covered birds, mainly eider ducks, guillemots and gulls were now coming ashore so badly affected that the RSPCA had to put most of them down.

Divers succeeded in attaching a second tow-line and, after 24 days of coping with all the hazards of the sea in some pretty foul weather, as well as all the irritating complications of national and commercial officialdom, the bow section of the *Eleni V* was towed to a deep water point 26 miles off Lowestoft. Navy divers used two and a half tons of explosive to blow it apart, vapourising and burning off the 1,100 tons of fuel it still contained in one mighty bang which was heard up to 40 miles away.

This is how a reporter on a local paper saw it: 'On board the frigate *Plymouth* with Royal Naval experts, Department of Trade officials, other Press and television men and the massed ship's company we saw the sea erupt from the first shock waves created by the two and a half tons of high explosives packed to the oil-laden hulk 26 miles off Lowestoft yesterday. Within seconds orange flames were licking from under the hulk and then there was this tremendous bang – I've never heard anything like it – and black smoke, orange flames and burning oil mushroomed 1,500 to 2,000 feet into the air. It didn't burn for long – within minutes the sea was calm and you wouldn't know anything had happened. The *Eleni* had gone – but the end was very spectacular.'

For seven years Yarmouth Borough Council battled to win £300,000 for the costs of clearing up that terrible oil slick along its coastline. The *Eastern Daily Press* reported,

'Local authorities were assured by the then Labour government that they would not suffer losses. But years of wrangling have so far led to the council receiving a little over a half of its original expenditure of £326,459. Now, councillors are being urged to accept terms being offered by solicitors acting for the shipping companies ... As part of the bargain Yarmouth council would have to agree not to make any more claims against the *Eleni V* or the *Roseline*.'

This was a remarkable shipwreck in that the pollution it produced caused a special inquiry to be ordered into all aspects of the Government's contingency planning for handling disasters at sea. Perhaps there were too many cooks spoiling the broth in dealing with oil spillage, but *The Times* quotes Mr Cecil Creber, the Board of Trade official in charge of the 24-day operation as saying, 'Not a step along the road has been wrongly taken. If I was faced with another tanker disaster tomorrow, I think I should take the same decisions.'

A Pirate on the Long Sand

In the *Daily Telegraph* of 26th May 1990 we are told:
'The Independent Broadcasting Authority is facing the
threat of legal action from one of its own local radio
stations, which has been caught up in a battle of the
airwaves to silence the pirate station Radio Caroline.' It
appears that the Spectrum Radio station had been assigned
the same frequency occupied by Radio Caroline – 558 on
medium wave – and was consequently drowned out by
Caroline's powerful level of transmission. Silencing Radio
Caroline is not an easy task it seems. But it has happened
twice – for two very short periods. Craig Seton, writing in
The Times of 21st March 1980 put it very neatly:
   'Radio Caroline, the original pirate radio ship, sank off
the Essex coast yesterday, silenced by the heavy seas that
were the only threat to its existence since it was outlawed
by the British and Dutch governments in the late 1960s.'
   This was not the first time the lifeboat was called out to
save lives from the *Mi Amigo*, the old Dutch coaster which
had been specially converted to a radio station, with a
lofty mast for its transmitter making it instantly recogniz-
able. Fourteen years previously, on 19th January 1966, a
vicious, snow-laden wind hit the radio ship so hard that it
broke from its moorings and ended up on the beach near
Chevaux de Frise Point at Great Holland. The lifeboat
service's inspector reported on the incident, concluding,
'The coxswain and his crew showed courage, determina-

The *Mi Amigo*, alias Radio Caroline, is battered on the beach during her first shipwreck in January 1966.

tion and skill in boarding the lifeboat in conditions of wind, sea and bitter cold which were the worst known for many years at this most exposed station.' The lifeboat could not itself make the rescue but had to stand by while the *Mi Amigo*'s men were brought ashore by the line rigged by the team operating the Life Saving Apparatus, better known as the breeches buoy.

It was not long before cheeky Radio Caroline was in position once again, 13 miles off the Essex coast east of Southend, because it was necessary to station the *Mi Amigo* outside the territorial waters of the United Kingdom to avoid prosecution. Twenty four years after it was blown ashore the ship and the station were being run by a crew of just four men who, on the fateful Thursday, 20th March 1980, included two men of East Anglian origin. One was Timothy Lewis from Snape, Suffolk and the other was Nigel Tibbles from Rayleigh, Essex. They may have been men of the modern age of pop-songs and soft-living but they certainly showed their metal when, for the second time, Radio Caroline went aground.

On this Thursday a gale sprang up; it became a storm that blew the *Mi Amigo*, anchor, cable and all off its mooring and on to the notorious Long Sand to the north-east – graveyard of so many ships. Here the anchor caught and held. The crew had to report their new position, but they did not really appreciate what danger they were in. The Coastguard did. They alerted the Sheerness lifeboat station and the *Helen Turnbill*, having just returned from a rough weather exercise, had hurriedly to turn out again for the real thing.

Out it went at full speed into the teeth of a force nine gale. The sea was so rough with short steep seas that the lifeboat was like a boxer taking a series of thumping jabs on the chin. Speed had to be reduced because the boat was shipping so much water. Through the Oaze Deep, into the Black Deep, and then, from the crest of a mighty wave the *Mi Amigo* was spotted lying on the Long Sand with the receding tide leaving it in only a few feet of water. Radio contact was made, help was offered, but these unusual sons of the sea and the air waves said they did not need immediate help as they were even then trying to get the pumps working in the hope that they would get off the sand as the tide rose.

They did not have the lifeboatmen's long experience of what could happen to a vessel on the Long Sand in such heavy seas. The lifeboat came up close to the stern of the

Mi Amigo and kept station there as both vessels were pitched and tossed about by the rollers sweeping across the sands. The coxswain told the Caroline crew, sweating still over the pumps, that they would be in serious trouble, not to say danger to life, if their ship sank in the rapidly rising tide. It became obvious to the Caroline boys that the pumps were not going to cope with the inrush of water into the badly leaking vessel. They accepted the offer of a lift shorewards from the lifeboat.

The *Helen Turnbill* then fell further astern of the *Mi Amigo* to assess the best way of getting near enough to take off the crew. The coxswain spotted that on the starboard side of the stricken ship there were rubber tyres suspended to act as fenders for supply ships. So he chose that side to make his approach and asked his men to judge their course and speed so that they would come alongside at the precise moment between the crests of two racing waves. It was a rescue fraught with immense danger because one error in the fine judgment of helmsman or engineer could lead to the lifeboat being smashed down on the *Mi Amigo*'s deck.

Patience and seamanship were the order of the day. Three times the *Helen Turnbill* attempted to run in but had to break it off. At the fourth attempt one man was grabbed before yet another wave crashed down on the deck. Round went the lifeboat in those awful seas, to approach the *Mi Amigo* five more times and come away at last with the second man. It was as they were about to pull away at full speed that the third man started running down the deck, carrying a bird in a cage. The lifeboat throttled back, the man jumped to safety, and a great wave lifted the lifeboat and slammed it against the ship's side. It took four more dangerous passes at the stricken vessel, now being overwhelmed by the waves, before the last disc jockey could be pulled to safety from the stanchion to which he

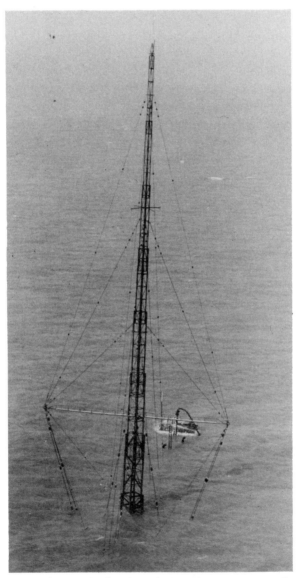

The pirate radio ship was finally silenced when the *Mi Amigo* sank in a storm in March 1980. (Reproduced by kind permission of the East Anglian Daily Times)

had been clinging for dear life. The very next wave lifted the *Mi Amigo* high, and it seemed to give a great sigh as it slipped down on to the sand in 25 ft of water.

Having taken the first disc jockeys ever to be saved from the sea back to Sheerness, the coxswain told the press, 'The operation to get the crew off took twelve hours. It was the hairiest rescue I have ever done.' The survivors were taken to the police station where they received the warmest hospitality. At the same time they were warned that they would be reported to the Director of Public Prosecutions under the Marine Broadcasting (Offences) Act of 1967 because the ship, albeit wrecked, represented a pirate radio station in the national waters of the United Kingdom!

The *Mi Amigo* still lies deep in the Long Sand, but anyone can switch on their radio and hear Caroline still sailing along on the air waves.

All Ashore!

The story of the *Wegro* started on the morning of Sunday, 27th April 1981, when a really ferocious storm was battering the Norfolk coast, with winds blowing at up to 50 miles an hour. The *Wegro*, registered in Dublin, had virtually completed its voyage from the Thames to Yarmouth, but it could not risk negotiating the harbour entrance in the force nine gale, especially as it was carrying fuel amounting to some 3,800 gallons of gas oil. It was travelling light, due to pick up a cargo of grain at Yarmouth for transport across the North Sea to Ghent. Being empty, its height out of the water made it all the more difficult to handle in the very strong wind. Captain Stanley Garland decided to anchor off the coast and ride out the gale.

The storm was so severe that the anchor could not hold; wind and the flooding tide forced the *Wegro* towards the beach. Even when her engines were set to full speed ahead she could not halt the drift back to the beach – and there she was left by the receding tide, broadside on to the sea front, across a heavy timber groyne. The *Wegro*'s plight sparked off a full-scale rescue alert under the aegis of the Yarmouth Coastguard Station. A helicopter was called up from Coltishall and the Gorleston lifeboat, *Khami*, was launched into what coxswain Richard Hawkins described as 'terrific seas'. Despite the extreme discomfort and the very real danger of their position the lifeboat stood by until the receding tide ruled out any further necessity for their services.

The burden of the rescue fell not on the helicopter but, most unusually, on the Gorleston Coast Rescue Company. This long-established but little credited organisation was set up solely to effect the rescue of shipwrecked sailors from the beach by means of lines, fired out to the wreck by rockets and attached to sheer legs on the beach so that a breeches buoy could be suspended, sent out to the wreck and hauled back with a survivor.

Though it had not been called upon to give a full service for the past 20 years, it went smoothly into action and brought ashore safely two young men who might be termed 'supercargo'. One was Keith Ralph, 15 years old, brother of the *Wegro*'s engineer, and the other was Nicholas Stanton, aged twelve, Captain Garland's nephew. It

While the *Wegro* was stranded on Yarmouth beach for several days awaiting a sufficiently high tide to refloat her, the captain and crew gave guided tours to sightseers in aid of the lifeboat funds.

was just a holiday voyage for them, but what an adventure they had to relate when they got back home! The five man crew declined to be saved, stayed with the ship, and simply climbed down to the beach at low tide.

There was a lot of head-scratching as to how the coaster, looming up on the beach as big as a couple of hotels and 170 ft long, was to be refloated. The captain, at a press interview, said that everyone was finally agreed that they would have to clear away the sand, dig out the groyne, inspect the *Wegro* for possible damage, and, if the ship was declared seaworthy, have bulldozers dig a great trench from the ship seawards. Mercifully, in the next week the weather improved and these proposals could be put in hand.

The *Yarmouth Mercury* of 1st May was not altogether confident of the outcome: 'The stranded coaster *Wegro* could become a summertime fixture on Yarmouth beach if efforts to refloat her on Monday end in failure.' While the *Wegro* waited for that crucial highest tide it was repaying the lifeboat service for its unstinted aid. Captain Garland confirmed that owner Tom Allsworth would be glad to allow guided tours of the stranded ship in return for donations to the lifeboat funds. A gangplank was organised up the steep side of the *Wegro* and soon scores of people had seen just what it was like to live and work at sea on a coaster, while ladies from the Lifeboat Guild provided the collection boxes. A good time was had by all and a worthy cause benefited considerably.

When the bulldozers had done their work and the tide was high the Yarmouth tug *Hector Read* made a tentative attempt to tow the *Wegro* clear. It moved just a few inches, which indicated the possibility of success when the tide reached its maximum height and the more powerful tug *Indomitable* could be brought into the battle on Saturday 2nd May, at a cost of more than £10,000.

The word went round that the effort to haul the *Wegro* off was to be made that evening and a constant trickle of people flowed to the best vantage points in brilliant sunshine as the tide swelled on a calm sea. Police were required to make sure that sightseers stood well back in case the massive wire towing hawser snapped and whiplashed across the beach. The tug *Eta* passed the hawser from the *Indomitable* to the *Wegro*, then, at 6.55 p.m. precisely the *Indomitable* took up the strain. There was a moment of heart-stopping tension, then the *Wegro* moved, slid into the excavated trench, gathered way, and in just four minutes it was out there on the briny, afloat again. The crowd applauded, motorists peeped their horns, the *Wegro* acknowledged their good wishes with a couple of hoots on its siren and one 'shipwreck' ended happily. The only people disappointed were the folk who had planned a day trip to Yarmouth on May Day to see this ship ashore – and the *Wegro* left them in the lurch by going two days early!

The Townsend Thoresen cargo ferry *European Gateway* capsized with the loss of five lives, after collision with another cargo ferry, within sight of Harwich in 1982. (Reproduced by kind permission of Essex County Newspapers Ltd.)

118

A Modern Tragedy

The tragedy of the *European Gateway* is so recent that it still affects the lives of the survivors and the relatives of those who were lost in the disaster. One would have imagined that, with all the modern aids to navigation and with the building of ships in such durable materials, there would be only the remotest chance of a shipwreck today. It is the uncertainty of the human element in the changing environment of the sea which still brings accidents and fatalities.

The *European Gateway*, a cargo ferry owned by Townsend Thoresen, was lost at around eleven o'clock on the night of Sunday 19th December 1982. In a gale, about two and a half miles off Harwich, it had collided with the *Speedlink Vanguard*, a British Rail cargo ferry. The *Gateway*, 3,949 tons, was outward bound to Rotterdam from Felixstowe with 48 trucks and trailers and a total of 70 people aboard, including the crew. The *Vanguard*, 5,555 tons, returning from Zeebrugge to Harwich, was loaded with containers and railway wagons, but the crew of 28 were the only people aboard. It reported that it had suffered damage in the collision but that it could make Harwich without assistance.

The *European Gateway*, on the other hand, was very seriously damaged. Within half an hour of the collision it was radioing that it was in imminent danger of capsizing. Just a few minutes after that it did fall on its side and the

36 crew and 34 lorry drivers had to climb out on to the uppermost side of the ship. There some of the men, probably those who could not swim, found what hand-holds they could on the swaying hull and waited stoically for possible rescue in the chilling wind and the darkness of a December midnight. Though they did not then know it, they were not in immediate danger of going down with the ship and drowning because the *Gateway*, struck amid-ships, had turned on its side, sunk as far as it could, and was now resting on a sandbank.

Other men were flung, or decided to jump clear of the ship, into seas which had only recently abated from the effects of a force ten storm to the conditions of a force six gale. Some of the crew had tried to lower a lifeboat, but the rapid listing of the *Gateway* gave them no time to complete the manoeuvre. They then scrambled into a few rubber life rafts which had floated clear. In their haste to get away from the doomed ship some of the men jumped one on top of another. It was not only the listing of the ship which had prevented the lowering of lifeboats; the bow of the *Speedlink Vanguard*, driving in at an angle of 45 degrees, damaged several of the lifeboats as it scraped down the side of the *Gateway*.

It was extremely fortunate that at that time of night, and in those difficult, stormy conditions, there were three small ships in the vicinity which could race to the rescue. They were the pilot boats *Patrol*, under Second Officer Wright, the *Valor* under Coxswain Lee, and a third launch under the control of Coxswain Pickering. Though there were ropes dangling from the *Gateway*, used by the ship-wrecked in their escape, which could easily have fouled the propellers, these little rescue ships went in time and again to snatch men from the sea and off the *Gateway* itself. When it was all over Captain Jack Hart, Superintendent of Pilots at Harwich, paid the rescuers this tribute: 'These men showed great courage. If they had not gone back again and again a lot more men might have perished. It was a very hairy operation.' Coxswain Lee picked up 28 survivors and three corpses. Two other men were later confirmed as dead. All the rest were rescued, suffering from exposure and shock, but fortunately without serious injury.

The three bodies were transferred to the Harwich lifeboat which had joined other boats and rescue helicopters with searchlights at the scene in a search which continued until names could be checked and every man accounted for. It continued through the day because one man was still missing, but was called off at dusk.

Captain Sharp explained at a press interview that the accident happened in a channel half a mile wide and more than 30 ft deep. 'There was plenty of water there for these two vessels to pass comfortably. It happens all the time without incident but I do not know the cause of this accident . . . Visibility was good and everything was working normally but I do not want to pre-empt the results of the investigation.'

At the public inquiry into the accident, which ran from 5th November 1983 until 4th August 1984, the captain of the *European Gateway*, Herbert McGibney told how he had tried to physically restrain some of the Dutch drivers on board because '. . . they were getting anxious for their lives and wanted to jump overboard.' One of the reasons for the ferry sinking so quickly was that three watertight doors had been left open. If they had been closed as required by regulation the auxiliary engine-room would have been flooded, but the ship would have stayed afloat and no-one would have died from drowning or exposure.

The finding of the Court of Inquiry eight months later was that both captains were to blame for over-complacency as the ships approached each other. *The*

Times sums it up: 'Captain Herbert McGibney of the *European Gateway* failed to keep a good lookout, tried to cross ahead of the *Speedlink Vanguard* when it was unsafe to do so, and was censured by the court. Captain John Bolton of the *Speedlink Vanguard* altered course to starboard when he should have reduced speed, and was admonished.'

The *European Gateway* was eventually successfully righted by a tug and towed into port, but the owners did not care to bring it into operation again and it was sold to a Greek company.

Bibliography

BATES, L. M., The Thames on Fire. 1985.
BENHAM, Hervey, Once upon a Tide. Rev. ed. 1971.
BENHAM, Hervey, The Salvagers. 1980.
CHURCHILL, Winston S., The World Crisis. 2nd ed. 1923.
KNIGHT, E. F., The Harwich Naval Forces. 1919.
MALSTER, Robert, Wreck and Rescue on the Essex Coast. 1968.
MALSTER, Robert, Saved from the Sea. 1974.
TEMPLE, C. R., Shipwreck! 1986.

Newspapers and magazines consulted include:
Chelmsford Chronicle (later Essex Chronicle)
Coastguard
Colchester Gazette
Daily Telegraph
East Anglian Daily Times
Eastern Daily Press
Eastern Evening News
Essex Countryside
Essex County Standard
Essex Weekly News
Harwich and Dovercourt Free Press
Illustrated London News
Ipswich Journal
Kent and Essex Mercury
Norwich Mercury
P.L.A. Monthly
Suffolk Chronicle
The Times
Yarmouth Mercury

Index

INDEX